Marc Déceneux

THE MONT-SAINT-MICHEL
stone by stone

Photographs by the author
Drawings by Maria-Luisa Levak - Atelier Zoupiotte
Cut-away diagrams in colour by Robert-Henri Martin

Editions OUEST-FRANCE

General structure of the monument

**The abbey of Mont-Saint-Michel is buiilt on the peak of a pyramid-shaped rock. The abbey church is built on the summit, on a platform made up of four crypts which completely surround the point of the hill.
The other buildings are disposed around it, terraced on the slopes.**

Below: plans at the level of the church and at the level of the crypts.
Right: axonometric cut-away diagram of the structures one above the other.
Drawings by Robert-Henri Martin.

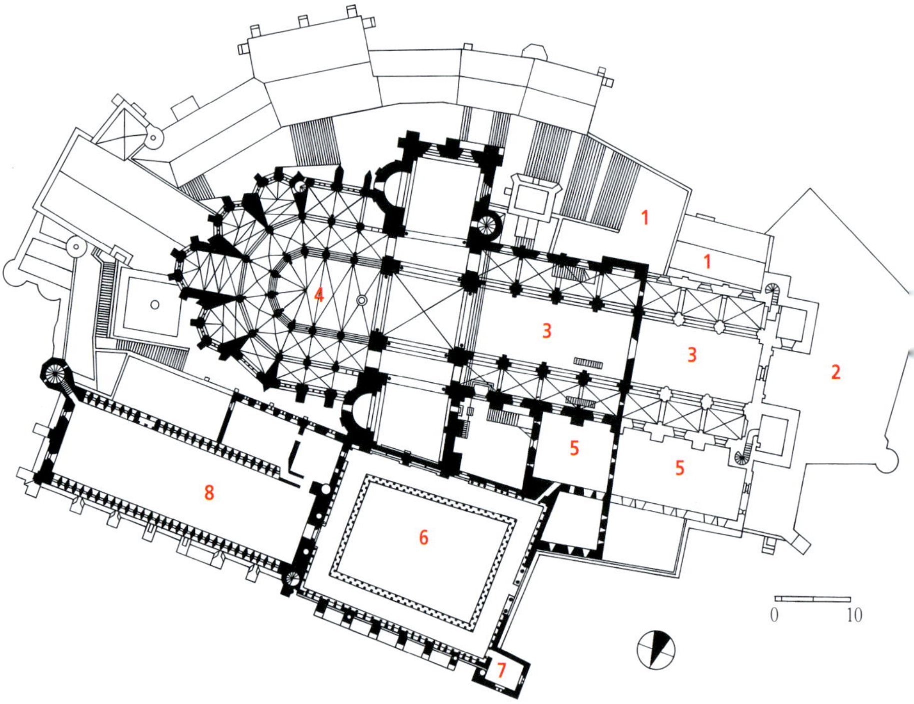

Captions of the plans and corresponding pages

1 : Terrace and hall of Saut-Gautier
2 : West terrace
3 : Romanesque church 18, 21, 30-38
4 : Flamboyant Gothic chancel 23, 57-60
5 : Dormitory 40
6 : Cloister 52-55
7 : Archive building 52
8 : Refectory 48-50
9 : Châtelet 12
10 : Hall of Belle-Chaise 13, 56
11 : Abbot's lodging 13
12 : Saint-Martin crypt 17, 21, 33
13 : Old ossuary 28
14 : Saint-Etienne chapel 28, 43
15 : No-longer extant south-west building 24, 43, 56
16 : Fleurs-de-lys hall 24, 42
17 : Robert de Thorigny's bedroom 43
18 : Romanesque ascending gallery 39
19 : Crypt of Notre-Dame-sous-Terre 26, 34
20 : Hall of the Promenoir 40, 44
21 : Devil's dungeon 46
22 : Crypt of Our Lady of the Thirty Candles 24, 33
23 : Hall of the Kinghts - Scriptorium 51
24 : Guest Hall 23, 47
25 : Crypt of the Big Pillars 58
26 : Kitchen garden above a cistern 63

SUMMARY

FROM THE SITE TO THE PROGRAMME

Photo André Mauxion.

THE NATURAL SETTING

Visitors to the Mont-Saint-Michel have always been struck with wonderment at sight of this fabulous piling-up of buildings that climbs the steep escarpments of the rock. In the face of this dizzying architectural feat, one inescapable question looms large in the mind: Why?

A big question requiring a long answer, for the simple truth is that time on the Mount is never measured the same as elsewhere. It starts with the violent convulsions which have shaped our land over 600 million years. The Hercynian folding of the primary era, raised mountains, which were planed down by erosion during the secondary era and broken up during the tertiary by see-saw movements of the earth to form isolated hills and peaks. The Mont-Saint-Michel, a cone of granulite 80 metres [262 feet] high, is one of these rocks like the island of Tombelaine 3 km [2 miles] to the north, and further away to the south-west, the Mont-Dol.

The bay where it stands, which covers 45,000 hectares [108,000 acres] is the scene of one of the biggest tides in the world. Twice a day, the broad movement of the Atlantic water-masses, concentrated into the funnel of the Channel and augmented by the water driven back by the

The Mount from the south-west. Left, the "Sea dyke". The polderizing of the bay from 1851 to 1933 joined forces with the natural sanding-up to make the Mount an island, which gives the monument its full significance. Work on an impressive scale is planned during the coming few years to ensure that the Mont-Saint-Michel remains an island.

barrier of the Cotentin, is set into motion by the attraction of the moon and the sun. At high water, during the twice-monthly spring tides, the rock is surrounded by an immense liquid plain; at dead low water, the sea can draw back as much as 18 kilometres [11 miles]. At such times the range from highest to lowest water reaches 15 metres [50 feet], i.e. the height of a five-storey building. When the tide is flowing, the sea rises at the impressive speed of 62 metres [203 feet] a minute - 1 metre [3'31/2"] a second! - and can do so considerably faster when low pressures and strong storm winds increase the height of the tide.

To that we can add storms, fogs, shifting sands... Men have always meditated on these strange and monstrous wonders. They have also given them an interpretation: what they have built is only the continuation of their dream.

Aerial view from the south-west.

The unusual land- and sea-scape of the bay, seen from the Grouin du Sud.

Let us look first at the naked rock: an immutable silhouette standing in a landscape in constant transformation. It evokes an indestructible stability, an enormous, eternal strength; around it stir the threatening, confused and dangerous forces of chaos.

It is also a vertical axis, linking together the three levels of the universe, the sky the earth, and the nether world, furnished by the imaginings of legendry with the tombs of dragons or giants. Axis of the world, that is to say a passage, an opening through which is established the communication between our world and that of the divine presences above.

But the Mount is also an island, a place cut off from the ordinary standards which govern time and space. And you can reach it only by means of a risky and uncertain crossing: the sea, which comes in, it is said, at the speed of a galloping horse, swallows up the imprudent traveller overtaken by fog; the quicksands, treacherous layers of firm sand in suspension above liquid muds, swallow up the unwary walker...

It was principally the Benedictines, who were installed in the rock since 966, who gave shape to these troubling ideas in a religious context. Through the magic of a gilded legend which they worked on to the grandiose fabric of the text which laid the foundations of medieval spirituality, the Book of Revelation, they attracted pilgrims in their thousands from the whole of Europe. They left the coast at Genêts, then headed westward, towards that disquieting west on which, in cathedral tympana, is fixed the gaze of the Blessed and the Damned at the Last Judgement. The crossing that they had to make, which brought them face to face with all the dangers of the bay, took them towards the Other World: a sort of dress rehearsal, as it were!

"The holy city, Jeruslaem, coming down from God out of heaven, having the glory of God..." (Book of Revelation).

Here, then, is the key: the Mont-Saint-Michel, in the unformulated medieval imagination, represents nothing less than the Jerusalem of the Apocalypse, descended from heaven to welcome the Blessed for eternity. According to the rules formulated by divine wisdom, the earthly city reflects the transcendental order which establishes the harmony of the celestial city. It will thus bring together the indissociable triad of Christian humanity: "those who work, those who fight, and those who pray". We shall find all that in this book: a village, a fortress, and a sanctuary. We shall make a rapid visit to the first two, and then explore the third more attentively, where the inspiration of the builders, architects and masons, reached its full flowering.

The village under the Ancien Régime, seen from the south. Copy of a model made around 1690 (original in the museum of relief-maps, Paris).

The existence of a village on the rock is connected with the development, as from 708, of the ever-growing success of a popular cult. Pilgrims must be housed and fed, and they do not leave without some pious object which they have acquired on the spot. We can thus consider that for twelve centuries a small, hard-working population on the Mount has been exercising the same trades: hotel business, catering, and sale of souvenirs.

It has been often repeated, following the lead of the architect Paul Gout, that the original town was on the northern flank of the rock, to receive the pilgrims who had set out from Genêts and passed via Tombelaine. Today is it impossible to continue to believe this unlikely hypothesis: recent archaeological probes have proved that no structure was ever built on that side, which is in any case inaccessible due to its steep slopes and battered by the prevailing winds. Simple common sense, and a few remains which are still visible (a Romanesque door in the ruins of the old convent of Saint Catherine, at the top of the main street on the left), make it clear that the built-up area has always occupied the south-east flank of the hill.

The research carried out by Edouard Corroyer and Paul Gout make it appear that the village was originally confined to the high part of the rock. But as of the XIVth century it must have extended to the base, as is shown by a miniature from the "Très Riches Heures" of the Duc de Berry. This extension can no doubt be laid at the door of the Hundred Years' War, since at that time the rock offered a safer refuge than the mainland, which was ravaged by incessant raids.

The general shape of the village was fixed at that time. It was structured around a main street, starting in the south and looping upwards to the entry of the monastery, which looks east. On to this main stem is grafted a maze of little streets and flights of steps which climb the slopes right to the foot of the abbey walls. The built-on part was organized on a mesh of narrow plots at right angles to the main street. Although the side walls of the houses were made of stone, for the most part taken from the rock itself, the façades were mostly half-timbered. This economical, flexible and modulable technique allows for ample lighting and, thanks to the corbelled construction of the upper storeys, an appreciable increase in living-space: space on the Mount is indeed measured in miserly amounts. Lastly, the very nature of the terrain ensures that some spaces were left free of construction; they rose in terraces, and it is there that the gardens were made. Thus, old documents tell us that there existed, on the arid rock, orchards, vegetable gardens, even minute pastures, since some of the inhabitants possessed one or two cows.

The Belle Epoque, with the economic progress due to the development of the tourist trade, was to make a fundamental change to the look of the village. Although the rigid and constraining pattern of the plots was hardly affected, most of the traditional houses disappeared, to be replaced by bourgeois edifices in stone, several storeys high. The town house of La Mère Poularde (1888) is one of the most impressive examples.

Present-day restorations are tending to give back to the little town of Mont-Saint-Michel a medieval, or post-medieval character, suitable to an urban complex which throughout the *Ancien Régime* was subjected to continual metamorphoses of detail.

The village seen from the east.

The parish church around 1390 ("Très Riches Heures du duc de Berry") (photo Giraudon).

As if to make clear the rustic nature of the little town, the pretty silhouette of the parish church stands halfway up the main street. It is dedicated to Saint Peter, and its origins are very old, since a charter of 1022 mentions it: "...the monastery of Saint Peter, prince of the Apostles, situated on the side of the hill." This text indicates that the church was founded by monks, either by the Benedictines, or more probably by the monastic community which occupied the site before 966.

The main part of the structure is made up of two parallel naves of two bays, the southern one narrower. This arrangement, which recalls that of the pre-Romanesque chapel of Notre-Dame-sous-Terre, in the heart of the abbey, appears to go back to the beginning of the XIth: the broad-bonded square pillars containing blocks set on end and the simply bevelled abaci recall the architecture of the crypts of the transepts of the abbey church (second quarter of the XIth).

The famous miniature of the "Très Riches Heures" of the Duc de Berry shows us Saint Paul's church as it looked around 1390. The twin naves appear as two adjoining buildings, each topped with a saddleback roof. The wider one, to the north, is slated and ends on the north with a windowless gable topped by a little pierced bell-tower; the other, which is tiled, shows a series of narrow openings in its south wall and, on the eastern side, a flat chevet in line with that of the northern sanctuary, pierced by two windows with a bull's-eye window above them, an arrangement which is a scaled-down copy of that of the abbey church transept.

In the XVth century, as the village is growing, the church is enlarged: the internal arcading is raised; the length of the naves is increased by the addition of small square chancels; another is added to the north of the main chancel. A three-storey square tower, with a saddleback roof in the Cotentin style, is built against the southern flank of the building; its ground floor, which opens on to the cemetery, makes a covered porch.

Finally, in the XVIIth century, the main chancel is enlarged , using a method which is frequently encountered in Counter-Reformation art, by an apse with cut-off corners on a vault which spans a public passage. The reredos of the high altar is no doubt later than this last alteration.

The parish church around 1690.

Recent restorations have set off to advantage the church and its riches: furniture, statues, tombstones, details of frescos and stained-glass windows, and above all the venerated silver statue of Saint Michael (1873), on view in the old south porch, on the ground floor of the bell tower.

Interior of the church after restoration (photo Luigi Levak).

The fortifications of the village

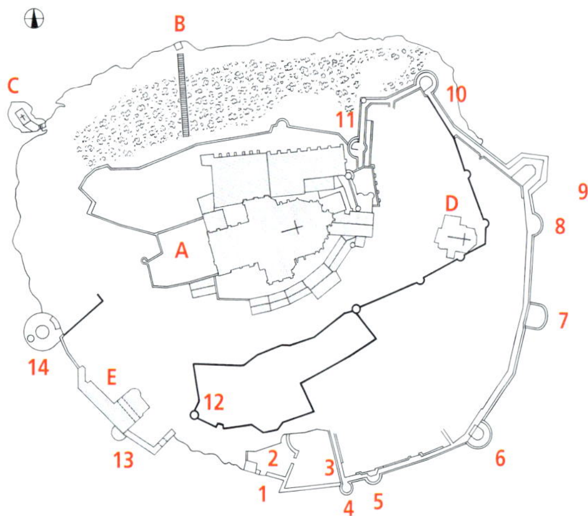

Fortifications of the village.

A: Abbey, B: Saint-Aubert fountain, C: Saint-Aubert chapel, D: Parish church, E: Fanils buildings

1: Avancée gate, 2: Boulevard gate, 3: King's gate, 4: King's tower, 5: Arcade tower, 6: Liberty tower, 7: Basse tower, 8: Half-moon (Chollet tower), 9: Boucle tower, 10: North tower, 11: Claudine tower, 12: La Pilette, 13: Fanils tower, 14: Gabriel tower

The solid line halfway up the slope shows the fortifications as they were before the XVth century, according to E. Corroyer and P. Gout.

The sketchy enclosing wall of the village around 1390.

It would seem that until the XIIIth century the village was not specially fortified. According to the sparse evidence of the chronicles, which is however backed up by architectural analysis, it was not until the years 1240-1250 that a first enclosing wall was built under the authority of the abbot Richard Turstin. These works, which were to receive a royal subsidy in 1256, allowed the enclosure of the little village which crowded round the foot of the abbey, near the summit of the rock. This undertaking included the north tower and the adjacent ramparts, which extended as far as the town gate, which at that time was situated near the parish church. For the rest, the old texts make it probable that the other defences comprised only wooden palisades.

Military works were also carried out during the last two decades of the XIVth century by abbots Geoffroy de Servon and

Link between the XIIIth-century ramparts (left) and those of the XVth century (right), between the Boucle tower and the North tower.

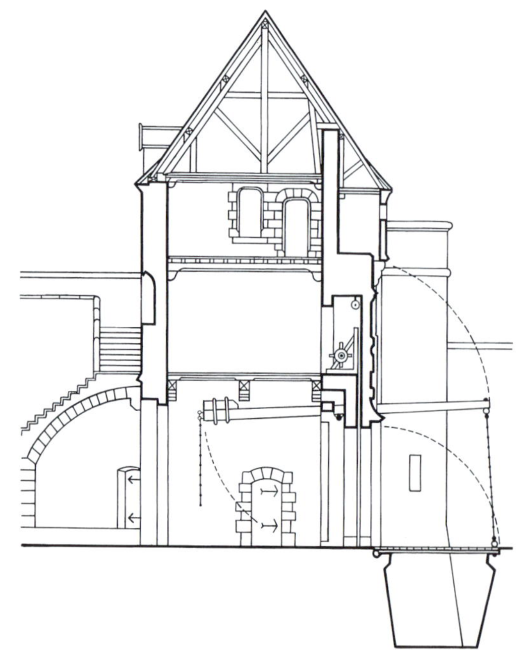

Right: section of the King's gate.

Pierre Le Roy. In 1386 a royal permit was issued allowing houses around the abbey to be pulled down if they were likely to interfere with the aim of the defenders. Small forts were also built on the rocky projections overhanging the south and west escarpments, which had not previously been defended. There are still a few remains to be seen, including the pretty corbelled bartizan of La Pilette.

In 1417, in the face of the threat from the English, abbot Robert Jolivet undertook an enormous series of fortifications surrounding the extra-mural parts of the village, before switching to support of the English cause. His work, which was taken

The Boucle tower around 1690.

further by captain Louis d'Estouteville, commander of the place in the king's name, kept the masons of the region busy until the middle of the XVth century. The final layout of the ramparts as we know them today was then firmly fixed, including in particular the King's gate, which closes off the main street with a ditch, a drawbridge, a portcullis and mighty doors in iron-banded oak.

A new series of defensive works was carried out after the Hundred Years' War in the reign of Louis XI. A noteworthy item dating from that period is the Boucle tower (1481), an artillery bastion equipped with low batteries and a central conduit to allow the escape of the smoke caused by firing. Its pentagonal layout, which ensures that it has a field of fire without blind spots, made it a revolutionary prototype which foreshadows by more than a century the classic fortification. Another identical construction existed in the present position of the Basse tower. It was already in ruins in the XVIIth century, and in the course of the XVIIIth was replaced by a small battery on a rounded platform.

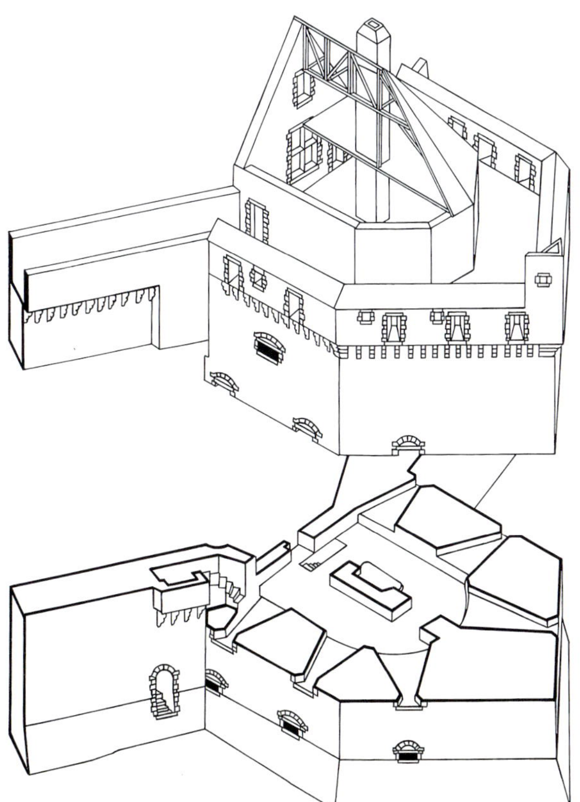

Left: horizontal axonometric section of the Boucle tower in its original state.

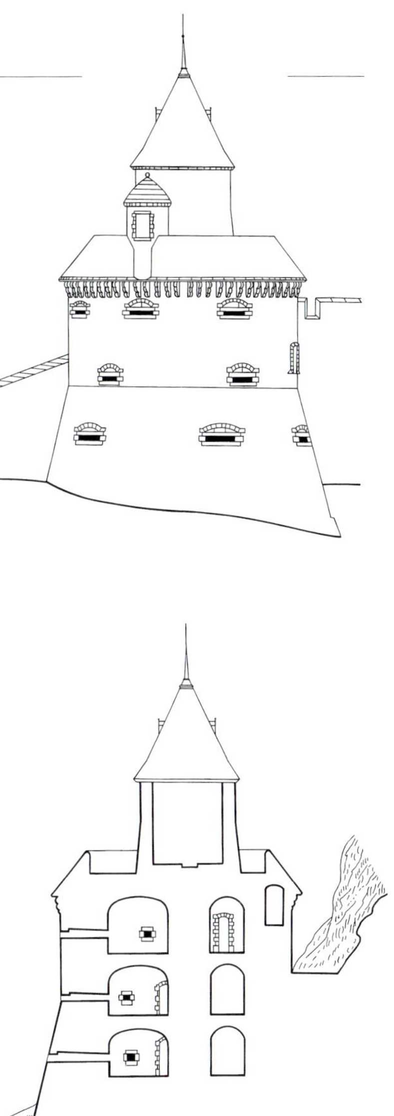

Elevation and section of the Gabriel tower.

Finally, the walls were once more strengthened at the beginning of the XVIth century. The Gabriel tower (from the name of its builder, Gabriel du Puy) on the south-west of the rock, was built in 1524, and the defences of the entry were multiplied; in 1525 you had to pass through three successive gates (the Avancée gate, the Boulevard gate and the King's gate) to enter the village.

The ramparts which surround the base of the Mont-Saint-Michel thus constitute a veritable anthology of medieval fortification. Vauban, who visited the Mount in 1689, could not find words enough to praise their perfection, in which he saw "a masterpiece, and mayhap the boldest, most consummate work in the world".

The abbey seen from the North tower. The fortified entrance to the monastery is both the culminating point and the command post of the ramparts.

The town walls link with those of the abbey, which are, as it were, their keep. There is evidence of fortifications there from the end of the Xth century, at which time duke Richard of Normandy had the Benedictine monastery which he had just founded there enclosed by stout walls. But the earliest remains which are still visible today are those of an enclosing wall at the foot of the abbey walls, on the southeast side, including in particular a fortified entrance in a square crenellated tower; the miniature of the "Très Riches Heures" shows it intact. It is probably an advanced fortification, set up in the middle of the XIIIth century, when the abbey entrance, originally on the west, was moved to the eastern side.

Advanced defences (XIIIth century) of the abbey around 1390 ("Très Riches Heures du duc de Berry").

But the military installations which we can still admire today date from the end of the XIVth century, when the Hundred Years War was in full spate. The XVth-century illuminations which show the Mount are works of imagination (the book of hours of Pierre II of Brittany, the duke of Bedford's breviary, Jean Miellot's book of the Miracles of the Virgin). However, they all agree in depicting the south front of the abbey, above the village, as a military wall, crenellated along its whole length.

The fact is that very extensive works were carried out by abbots Geoffroy de Servon (1363-1386) and Pierre Le Roy (1386-1411). From a crenellated terrace built in the XIIIth century in the south-west corner, there stretch from west to east the main abbey buildings, crowned with watch-walks, the Perrine tower, a square block of six storeys where the soldiers were quartered, and finally the Châtelet, an extremely elegant fortified gate built in 1393.

This "châtelet" (small fort) is a square building, the ground floor of which is pierced by a vaulted passage which houses the Gouffre staircase, which leads to the Hall of Guard and was defended by a portcullis and firing holes designed to keep any assailant under the threat of direct fire. Its façade is framed by two slim towers carried on *cul-de-lampe* corbelling which is embedded in the buttresses, and given animation by courses of different colours. The whole is topped by a crenellated platform.

In front of this building is a barbican, a projecting work crowned by a watch-walk and opening, on the north and east, via pendant doors (doors pivoting on a horizontal axis at lintel level). This stronghold is itself dominated by the platform of the châtelet and the crenellated walk which joins the latter to the gable of the Merveille.

Once past these defences, you still had to get through a gate which divided the Hall of Guard into two parts, and then a second barring access to this hall from the Grand Degré staircase which leads up to the church (these gates, built by Pierre Le Roy, were later replaced by real fortified walls, which can be seen in the interior of the model of the Mount which was made around 1690 and is kept in the museum of relief-maps). Lastly, the staircase itself was defended by a portcullis, controlled from a bridge running between the church and the abbey buildings; the grooves in which it slid can still be seen.

The abbey fortifications were thus powerful, and made the monastery impregnable at that time, when artillery knew only direct fire and not ballistic fire. The show of force represented by this military architecture impressed its contemporaries, who were able to take it as a model: the forts of Fougères (XVth century) or of Trécesson (around 1400) give evidence of imitation of the prestigious prototype represented by that of Mont-Saint-Michel.

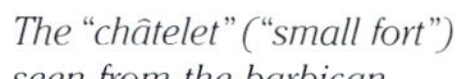

The "châtelet" ("small fort") seen from the barbican.

The south front of the abbey in 1400. Drawing by Pierre Belliard from information supplied by the author, coloured by Robert-Henri Martin. Inset: the same view around 1690.

The fortifications we have just described make the monastery which crowns the rock into a real fortified castle. This picture reminds us that the abbey is a seigniory, and the abbot its seignior. The gibbet, a major symbol of feudal power, has disappeared (it stood to the left of the town gate, where the bus-stops now are), but the abbey court has been preserved: it is the superb hall of Belle-Chaise, built in 1257, above the Hall of Guard where the abbey is entered, and which has been brought back to its former splendour by recent restorations.

The other element which testifies to the seigniorial power of the abbot is the abbot's lodging. The rule of Saint Benedict lays down as a principle that the abbot should share the life of his monks and, in particular, sleep in their dormitory. Robert de Thorigny, in the second half of the XIIth century, was the first to free himself from this constraint: the burden of his administrative duties made it necessary for him to lead a separate life, and he therefore had a separate apartment built, outside the enclosure, in the western parts of the monastery (see page 42)

But it is at the end of the XIVth century that an enormous lodging for the abbot was built by Geoffroy de Servon and his successor Pierre Le Roy, on the southern flank of the abbey. The work was begun in 1374 and finished in 1400. Its principal element is a long row of buildings, resting on high embanked foundations, parallel with the high church from which it is separated by the Grand Degré staircase, but to which it is joined by suspended bridges.

To the east, a large five-storey tower constitutes the main body. It has a broad projecting façade, reinforced by three large, flat buttresses; these latter bear the wall of the upper storey, which is slightly corbelled and rests on four pointed arcades carried by the buttresses and by narrow embedded columns supported by consoles. It is known as "the Abbot's tower".

Next, a shallower, lower wing stretches to a second tower, built in the same way as the Abbot's tower; however, it is less broad, and has only two buttresses and two arcades, with a single intermediary corbelled column. It is know as the Saint Catherine tower. The ensemble is topped with crenelated watch-walks, that of the central wing being overlooked by those of the towers.

This impressive palace is derived, as far as its shape is concerned, from one of the major works of civil architecture of the XIVth century, the Popes' Palace at Avignon, and more particularly from the western wing of it, that is to say the personal lodging of Benedict XII, which was built between 1335 and 1340. Here we find the same general approach: crenellated walls the upper parts of which are corbelled and carried on arcades which accentuate the effect of verticality, and an alternation of long façades and higher, square projecting towers.

Without going into detail, the two constructions show very similar internal layouts, and have significant points in common where their proportions are concerned.

It is of course true that there is nothing particularly innovatory about using the "Old Palace" of Avignon as a point of reference. The abbot's lodging of Mont-Saint-Michel is contemporary with important constructions which are much more advanced, like Pierrefonds. But the Norman adaptation of the papal château is evidence of the important place which the Mount held in the history of important architectural trends in Europe. It is also evidence of the pride of the abbots who ruled the monastery.

Before it was drastically changed in the XVIIIth and XIXth centuries, then restored between 1939 and 1955, the abbot's lodging was the subject of an important series of transformations at the beginning of the XVIth century. The abbot Guillaume de Lamps added an extra wing on the west, to which leads a graceful corbelled staircase-tower on the outer façade, and then heightened the whole ensemble to obtain an upper storey on the same level as the church. This upper level communicated with the south door via a pretty pierced covered gallery, which has now disappeared, and with the south transept via a wooden bridge which has been restored.

All these buildings, as well as the wing known as "the Bailliverie", between the Abbot's tower and the entrance building, which was given over to the management of the abbey's temporal affairs, are today shared between the administrative services of the monument and the monastic community, reconstituted in 1969 by father Bruno de Senneville.

Section of the Abbot's tower.

Left: the bridge over the Grand Degré links the church to the abbot's lodging. The openwork building in the foreground is a cistern (beginning of XVIth century).

THE WORK-SITE

Gift of the duchess Gonor to the abbey of Mont-Saint-Michel. "Cartulary of the Mont-Saint-Michel", Avranches municipal library ms 210 (photo Avranches municipal library).

Decision and financing

Architecture is never an innocent art. It brings about the transposition into stone of feelings, of ideas, of beliefs, in other words everything on which human society is based. A monument, especially if it is large and prestigious, is thus a symbolic emblem in which a society - or at least its leaders - proclaims its identity and its values.

Which means that the construction of the abbey of Mont-Saint-Michel is intimately linked with history. Look for instance at these few co-incidental happenings:

— 867-933: The Mont-Saint-Michel becomes Breton; building of Notre-Dame-sous-Terre.

— XIth century: Normandy comes to the fore as the most dynamic European state; building of the Romanesque church and monastery.

— 1204: Conquest of Normandy by Philippe Auguste, king of France; building of La Merveille.

— 1450: Liberation of Normandy at the end of the Hundred Years' War; building of the Gothic chancel.

— 1870: IIIrd Republic: France is burning with a desire for revenge after its defeat in the conflict with the German empire; the abbey is restored and crowned with a statue of the Archangel by an anticlerical State...!

Those in political power are thus often a factor in the decision to build a great monument. They are also, as a result, the first financial backers, either by a gift of money such as king Philippe Auguste made for the building of La Merveille, or by the offer of stone-quarries (the Chausey islands, given in 1022 by the duke of Normandy), or of tracts of forest for the structural timber, or of lands to provide income.

The second source of financing for the site is supplied by gifts made by the faithful. It is the custom, in fact, that every pilgrim, from the humblest to the most powerful, should make an offering appropriate to his means to the Archangel. Many medieval wills thus include clauses gifting money to places of pilgrimage which the testator has visited in his lifetime.

Finally, the third source of revenue comes from the capital gains produced by the monastery's feudal and landowning domain. Over the centuries, the abbey has built up a productive capital of priories, of farms, of mills, of forests and of lakes, to which should be added the various dues owed by its vassals for one reason or another.

The men

As today, a major medieval building site is the work of a very hierarchical organization. At the top it is reigned over by a double management: the proprietor and the site manager. This latter is the architect - often a layman - responsible for the technical realization of the functional and symbolic programme conceived by the sponsor, that is to say the abbot, surrounded and advised by his more knowledgeable monks. The site manager has to conform to a set of specifications which leave him but little room for manoeuvre. The romantic concept of the "artist" had no currency in the middle ages, and the relationship between the creator of the forms and the site managership was laid down canonically by the instructions of the second Nicene council (787): "The composition of religious pictures is not left to the inspiration of the artist; it belongs to the principles laid down by the Catholic Church and to religious tradition. Only the technical skill belongs to the painter, the composition belongs to the Fathers..." This text, which governs the liberty of the painter, applies of course with its full force to the site manager.

In order of importance, the stonemason is just below the site manager. This highly qualified craftsman has a certain amount of intellectual education: he must be able to read and interpret the architect's drawings, , and make correct use of the working plans and the templates. Every stonemason has his personal mark - the famous "jobber's mark" - which he engraves on every block he prepares. The site manager thus has the opportunity to judge of the quality of his work and to pay him "for the job". It sometimes happens that a stonemason is responsible for a team and in authority over other masons, in which case they engrave their master's mark. This was probably so in the construction of the small fort, which was put up very quickly (which presupposes a large number of workers) and where there is only one type of mark to be seen.

The other aristocrat of the site is the carpenter. No old roof-frames have been preserved in the abbey. However, old illustrations show us slender roofs with daring spans, which enable us to imagine the skill and virtuosity of the monastery's medieval craftsmen. The carpenters working today on the restoration sites (the Belle-Chaise and Saut-Gautier halls) are carrying on the admirable tradition of their remote predecessors.

After the mason, who lays the stones, come the roofer and the mortar-mixer, who prepares the cement of lime and sand: the importance of mortar in medieval building (see following chapters) makes this technician's rôle a crucial one. Finally comes the rank and file of labourers, workhands, carriers of stone and water.

The accounts of the abbey site have disappeared, perhaps in the 1944 fire which destroyed Saint Lô, where the Mount's archives had been transferred at the time of the Revolution. So we shall never know the names of those who, over the centuries, have contributed to the great work. The only ones who have not been forgotten are the monk Gervais Provost, site chief of the chancel at the end of the XVth century, master Robert and master Jehan, the sculptors of the cloister which had been designed by dom Garin, and lastly a certain Juhel, no doubt a stonemason, who at the beginning of the XVIth century carved his name in the stone of the arches which support the terrace of the Saut-Gautier.

Jobbers' marks on the west terrace.

Left: construction of the temple of Jerusalem, Avranches municipal library ms. 2 (photo Avranches municipal library). A stonemason, standing on scaffolding supported by a putlock, is ramming home the stone he has just laid with the heel of his cutting tool (see technical aspects page 19).

Below: carpenters at work on the Saint-Gautier building in 1996.

Saint-Martin crypt. The opening of the apse is made up of two perfect geometrical shapes: a square and a semi-circle, symbols of the earthly world and of heaven. The sanctuary thus represents the universe. on reduced scale. These shapes have the same significance in the illuminations: right, an angel, in the celestial part, brings inspiration to Saint Augustin in the earthly part. The haloed head of the latter is on the borderline between the two worlds because of his quality as a saint. Avranches municipal library ms. 75 (photo Avranches municipal library)

The temple, divine dwelling and meeting-place between God and man, must above all be built according to the mysterious rules on which the harmony of creation is founded. For the Scriptures tell us that God created everything "with number, weight and measure".

Now, the mental universe of medieval man was organized around ternary structures. So he perceived the world around us in terms of the three aspects of the material, the intellectual and the spiritual. This cipher grid allows a complete reading of the intentions which were ruling when the architectural work was being designed.

On the spiritual plane, there is first of all number, a pure idea which belongs to the realm of the non-created. The medieval commentators of the Holy Scriptures explored the symbolic content of numbers to the point of dizziness, and made a real language out of them. ONE indicates divine unity, absolute perfection; THREE is the number of the divinity defined as a trinity; FOUR represents the created world (the elements, the cardinal points, the evangelists, etc.). These last two combine to make SEVEN (3+4) and TWELVE (3x4) which express in various ways the divine presence within the creation or the allegiance of the universe to its creator. A multitude of other numbers are thus loaded with meaning and can be put together in an inexhaustible number of combinations. In the whole abbey, the sequence of levels, of bays or of pillars forms part of this holy arithmetic.

On the intellectual plane, number is translated by shape, which the eye perceives directly but which has no physical existence. FOUR, for example, generates the square, the symbol of the earthly world (the Earth is flat and is a quadrilateral). Unity is expressed by the circle, on which every point is equidistant from the centre and which, because there is no break in its contour, leads to the idea of perpetual motion around a unique and immutable axis; the circle thus evokes divine perfection and represents the heavens, God's abode, (or sometimes, earthly Paradise, the ideal world of the beginning).

Lastly, on the material plane, the shape generated by number will itself generate the layout of the monument thanks to the skill of the architect. He is required to combine the basic geometric shapes according to precise rules of harmony. The ratio of 1 to 6, for example, defines a long rectangle which symbolically expresses the proportions of the human body, but also those of Noah's Ark according to the book of Genesis; this ratio is to be found in the ground plan of the central nave of the abbey church. More complex is the famous Golden Number, inherited from Antiquity, which establishes a relation of harmony between two measurements, the ratio of the smaller to the larger being the same as that of the larger to the whole. It is formulated thus: $A/B=(A+B)/A$, and its mathematical solution is $(1+\sqrt{5})2=1.618$.

 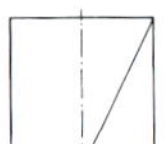 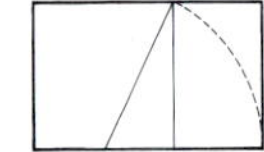

Geometrical construction of the Golden Number: the diagonal of the half-square, rotated on to the length, defines a rectangle in golden proportion.

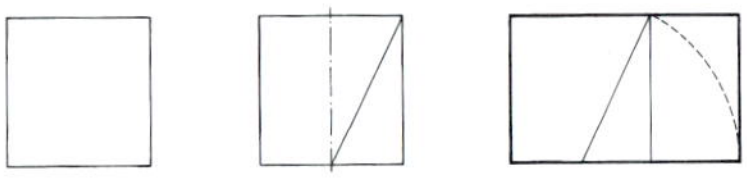

Right: each bay of the Romanesque nave is formed of two golden rectangles one above the other. The upper one gives the same golden proportion to the clerestory of the triforium.

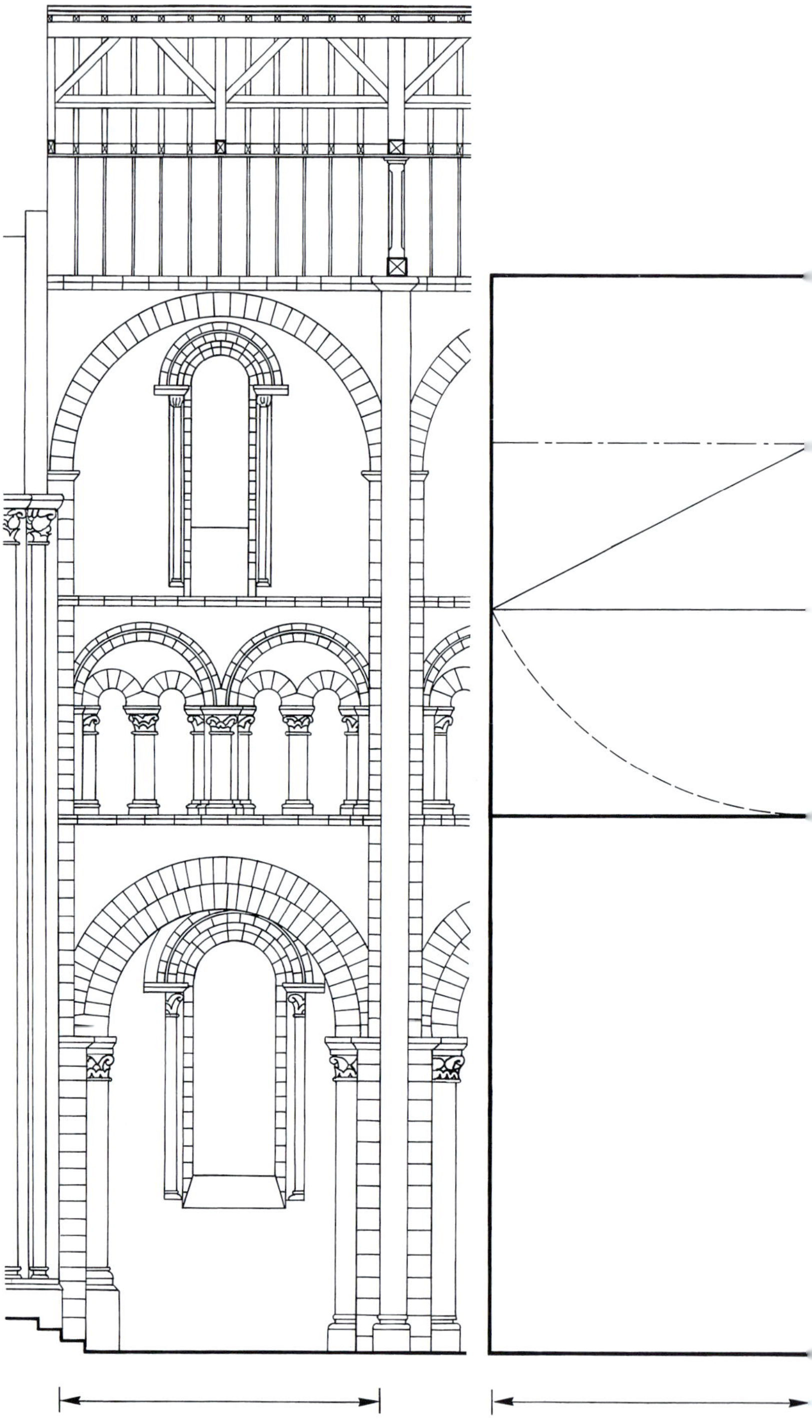

The Golden Number can be found in many places in the abbey, particularly in the bays of the nave of the church.

These regulatory outlines, easily drawn on paper, must be reproduced in full size on the site, to mark out both the plan and the elevations. each element of the building being prepared on the ground. For that purpose, it is necessary to lay out a grid on the ground, that is to say a regular pattern of squares which will serve as a point of reference for chocking. To achieve this all that is necessary is to have available a rope which will act as a compass but also as a square: regularly placed knots mark out twelve intervals; these must be divided into three sequences (3, 4 and 5 intervals). and folded to form a triangle; by application of Pythagoras's theorem, the figure obtained will be a right-angled triangle. The drawing opposite shows the stages of marking-out the grid using this method which was familiar to the masons of the Middle Ages.

Pythagoras's theorem: "In a right-angled triangle, the square on the hypotenuse is equal to the sum of the squares on the other two sides." This can be verified in the triangle 3/4/5: 52(25)=32(9) + 42(16).

Below : Pythagoras's triangle (somewhat approximately represented!) Avranches municipal library ms. 235 (photo Avranches municipal library).

Right: marking out the grid on the ground using the knotted rope.

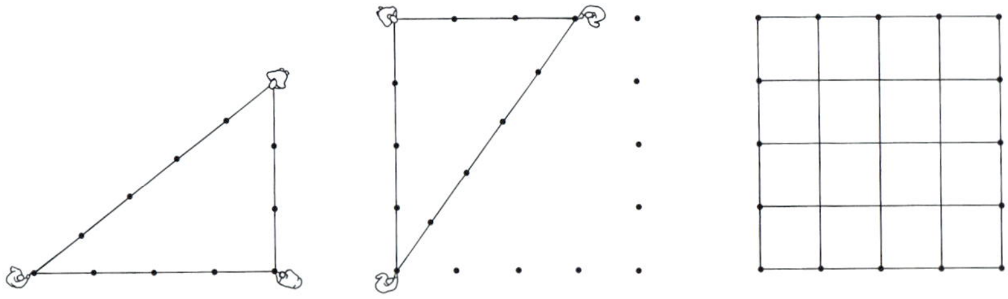

Cutting up granite, Note extraction in successive leaaves and the traces of lines of mortice-slots.

With the exception of occasional use of rare materials (Caen stone and English fossil-bearing limestone in the cloister), the main bulk of the abbey is built in granite, a hard stone formed from quartz, feldspath and mica. Except for a few rubble stones taken from the Mount itself, and the high parts of the chancel, made of Breton granite from Fontanelle, nearly all the stone comes from the Chausey islands, 35 kilometres (22 miles) off shore. The blocks were carried on barges as the tides permitted.

The quarrying of this stone was done by rows of slots cut in the living rock along its strata. Wedges pushed into these holes broke the main mass up into large leaves which were subsequently cut up. Shaping was carried out as far as possible at the point of quarrying in order to make transport easier.

The walls of the abbey show how the techniques of stone preparation developed over the centuries. In the pre-Romanesque period (Xth century) they are of small dimensions, broken with the hammer or shaped with a pick. In the Romanesque period (XIth and XIIth) the blocks are more regular; they are cut and roughly shaped with the pick, and their surface is then dressed with the adze or laye (a sort of hatchet). In Gothic times (XIIIth to XVth) dimensions are larger and the surface is dressed with a toothed laye (a hatchet with a toothed edge), which leaves it looking smooth and well-finished.

The other basic material of the site is lime. Quicklime, obtained by calcination of limestone at 900° or 1,000° C, is then slaked with water; one part of this slaked lime, mixed with three parts of washed sand, produces the mortar, to which cow-hair is sometimes added to give better adhesion.

Lime mortar has a rôle as a binder between the stones, but its principal function is that of damper: its relatively flexible and elastic nature ensures that charges and thrusts are distributed evenly within the masonry. Roman mortars, which were extremely hard, turned a monument into a monolith; those of the middle ages, on the other hand, allow settling and deformation to be absorbed.

Finally, water is indispensable to building. On the rock, which had only one spring, and that with limited flow, they built cisterns to stock rainwater, which, as everyone knows, is not lacking in our region.

All these materials are hoisted to the summit of the rock by means of highly developed lifting apparatus, the "gin" and the "squirrel-wheel" or hoist, which give very big reduction ratios. The large blocks are hung from "she-wolves", articulated tongs which grip tighter the heavier the load.

Once the stones and the tubs of mortar are on the spot and ready to be used, they are taken up the scaffolding which is built up at the same time as the walls. Putlock holes left in the masonry accommodate beams, the projecting ends of which carry platforms where the masons can work in complete safety.

The windlass-crane and its cart (XIXth century) in the old ossuary.

The same system in miniature (Douarnenez port-museum).

From left to right: two types of pre-Romanesque bond (crypt of Notre-Dame-sous-Terre, around 900, and Saint-Etienne chapel, around 995) Romanesque bond (abbey church, nave, middle of XIth century), Gothic bond (châtelet, around 1390. Photograph André Mauxion). Note the narrowness of the joints in this last picture: Gothic architecture, based on the rigidity of its structures, limits the use of mortar, which is a compressible material.

Groined vaults in the south side-aisle of the nave. Note the marked sag of the ribs.

Filled arch. XVth-century hall beneath the west terrace.

The walls of the Middle Ages were built on the principle of filled masonry. Fieldstone rubble buried in lime mortar is placed between two parallel rows of visible stone which also serves as shuttering. The XIth-century arches, for instance, in the south side-aisle of the nave, clearly show this method of construction.

Romanesque vaults, such as one can see in the abbey, are of three types: the barrel-vault is a continuous half-cylinder the weight of which rests on the whole length of its supporting wall; the groined vault is formed by two barrel-vaults which meet at right-angles; the semidome vault is half a cupola, that is to say a quarter-sphere. They are built on formwork: wooden vaulting mounted on a frame serves as a mould; on this is poured mortared rubble, which adopts its shape. Once the mortared rubble is dry, the formwork can be removed. The disappearance of the painted rendering of some vaults (the Saint Martin crypt) has revealed the imprint left by the planks of the formwork.

These vaults, which stay up because of their solid mass, have to be very thick. They are therefore very heavy, and produce considerable lateral thrusts. To counteract these, the supporting walls are very thick, with few openings, and reinforced on the outside by enormous buttresses.

However, these precautions do not avoid the deformations which occur because of the elasticity of the mortar; the groined vaults of the side-aisle of the nave have contracted to the point where they have the shape of a basket-handle arch. They have also, by pushing sideways, caused a bulge in the nave wall, seen from the inside. The barrel-vault of the south tran-

Barrel-vault in the hall of the Fleurs-de-Lys. Note the imprint of the formwork.

South arm of the transept.

sept has sagged down onto itself, and in so doing, has cut into the opening of the bull's-eye window.

Nevertheless, the site managers of Mont-Saint-Michel, in Romanesque times, were able to think up clever techniques to control all these movements. The southern arm of the transept and the Saint Martin crypt which serves as its base are each roofed with a barrel-vault of gigantic span (9 metres!) [30 feet!]. From one level to the next, the two superimposed barrel-vaults are crossed. The weight, which is thus shared between all four walls, is also chanelled by relieving arches incorporated in the masonry on both levels. The construction is thus, even if the fact is not visible, nothing but a gigantic assembly of pillars, whose equilibrium is due to the extreme concentration of their charge, which stabilizes them and allows them to oppose the thrust of the vaults.

This use - this extremely well thought-through use - of relieving arches constitutes an extraordinary attempt to localize charges and thrusts, and thus foreshadows - more than a century ahead of time - the technical principles which will be the foundation of Gothic architecture.

Above: section of the south arm of the transept and the Saint-Martin crypt.

Right: relieving arch framing the apse of the south arm of the transept.

Around the year 1100, a Norman invention is to bring about a veritable revolution in architecture: intersecting ribs, the first examples of which can be seen in the churches of Lessay and Durham, and, on the Mont-Saint-Michel, in the hall known as "Le Promenoir". The idea, seized upon by the architects of the Ile-de-France, will give birth in the middle of the XIIth century, to Gothic architecture (chancel of the abbey church of Saint Denis, consecrated in 1144).

The basic principle is as follows: the Romanesque vault, which was a thick block all in one piece, is replaced by an articulated series of slender vault-segments carried by permanent formwork, a framework made up of crossed stone ribs around a central key. The light thrusts exerted by these mini-vaults cancel one another out from one section to the next. The total weight, considerably reduced, is supported by the ribs, which concentrate it on spring points, between which the wall is no longer a supporting wall.

Of course, the charge transmitted by the arches will exert a lateral thrust on the supports; to counteract this, all that is needed is to build a buttress on the outside, or better still a flying buttress. This component, which saw the light of day on the Parisian sites around 1180, consists of two parts: the abutment is a heavy solid block, erected at some distance from the wall, the stability of which is further reinforced by the weight of a pinnacle, a stone spire which is also solid. An arch is attached to the abutment, which rises to meet the wall at the point where it receives the thrust of the interior vaulting. The curve of pressure exerted by the vault is prolonged through the arch and absorbed in the immovable masonry of the abutment. The flying buttress is thus, in Michelet's words, "the cathedral's crutch".

Elegance and lightness of Gothic vaulting: intersecting ribs in the Guest Hall.

Structure of a vault on intersecting ribs.

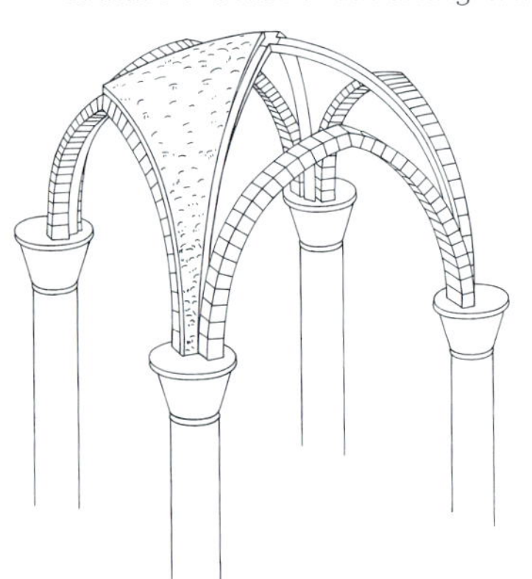

It can be noted that at Mont-Saint-Michel, as is the case of a number of large Gothic buildings, the arch which receives the thrust is matched by a higher arch which quite obviously has no rôle as a buttress. This supplementary arch has a triple function: it ensures that the top of the walls is not affected by movements of the roof caused by wind pressure; it ensures that it will not fall outwards if there is a fire in the roof frame; and lastly, it ensures that rainwater runs off in a controlled fashion, since the top of it is hollowed out to form a gutter.

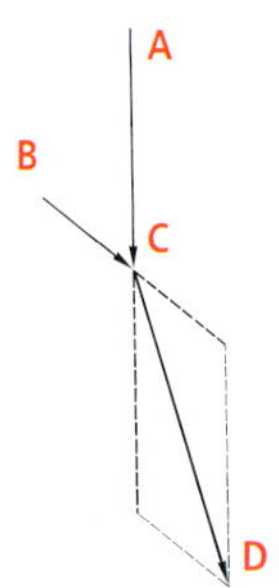

Theoretical path of resultant forces:

The arrow AC represents the weight of the upper masonry, the arrow BC represents the sideways thrust of a vault. The downward path of the weight will follow the arrow CD.

It was obviously difficult, on the steep slopes of the rock, to build flying buttresses, since their abutments would have had to be of an exaggerated height. Only the chancel of the church has them, therefore. The architect of the eastern building of La Merveille was also faced with the problem of buttressing ribbed vaults. The solution which he conceived brilliantly exemplifies all the genius of Gothic architecture.

Diagrammatic interior elevation and section of the east building of La Merveille.

The flamboyant chancel. Section of the ambulatory and of a radial chapel.

In the Guest Hall, on the first floor, the ribs of the vault do not rest on the wall, but on internal buttresses, continued on the other side by external buttresses. Although the fact is not visible, these masses are true buttress-walls, each of which is ballasted by the concentration of the weight of the upper storey, achieved by relieving arches thrown from one buttress to the next. The wall as a whole is thus made up of a series of parallel leaves, as it were like those of a radiator; the lateral pressure exerted by the relieving arches ensures both the stiffening and the solidarity of these leaves. On this rigid framework, which tends to act as a single block, the wall of the upper storey is built in overhang towards the interior. The counteracting moment caused by this imbalance neutralizes the pressure of the vault and the resultant of the forces in play is brought back practically to the vertical.

This example enables us to feel the extent to which Gothic architecture is a matter of a dynamic technique, controlling the balance of opposing but complementary forces. In that it is distinct from Romanesque architecture, a static art which opposes masses to the inert weight of other masses.

Sculptured panels of the old choir-screen.

Painted decoration in the hall of the Fleurs-de-:Lys.

Before we undertake a detailed visit to the monuments of the abbey,there is one preparatory measure that we must take: we must, from the very outset, exert all our imaginative capacity to re-create, as we view the huge, unadorned halls, the multi-coloured splendour which gave them a rich décor.

To start with, the furniture has completely disappeared, with the exception of a few rare items among which we can note the panels (XVIth century) of the old chancel screen. Three subjects are treated in them: the Temptation, the four Evangelists, and Christ arising from limbo. These bas-reliefs, which are mediocre in their execution, nevertheless have the merit of having retained some of their old polychrome finish.

Here and there in the monastery there are still remains of some of the old painted décor: false bonded stones in the crypt of Our Lady of the Thirty Candles, a scattering of fleurs de lys and arches (XIIIth) in a Romanesque hall recently rediscovered under the western terrace. It has also proved possible to save a large storiated fragment in the ruins of the XIIIth-century infirmary, which collapsed in 1811: it treats of the theme, very well-known in the middle ages, of the Three Dead Men, illustrating a moral story used by preachers. This moving relic can be seen in the hall of the Almonry. These few poor remains help us to imagine the colours which covered the walls: exposed stone, which is so much appreciated today, is a pure XXth-century fantasy.

Mention must also be made of the tiled floors made of small enamelled bricks which decorated the floor with rosettes, with multi-coloured foliation, or, as in La Merveille, the arms of France and of Castille, in homage to the mother of Saint Louis. These floor-tiles were broken and thrown away during the period of the central house. It was feared that the prisoners might use them as ammunition in case of a mutiny; they were replaced by the large slabs of grey stone which we can see today.

Finally, we must imagine the stained-glass windows ablaze with a thousand colours. Those of the chancel showed the history of Saint Aubert, and the king of France (Louis XI) surrounded by the twelve peers. In the Hall of Guard, the bull's-eye window carried the royal arms with the winged stag. Finally, in the Romanesque nave was a big window depicting the Passion. A few fragments of it were found in 1875 by the architect Edouard Corroyer. They have since disappeared, but the drawings which Corroyer made of them enable us to know what they were like; they show faces with enormous eyes which seem to be contemplating The Beyond.

False stonework in the crypt of Our Lady of the Thirty Candles.

Parts of a fresco from the old infirmary.

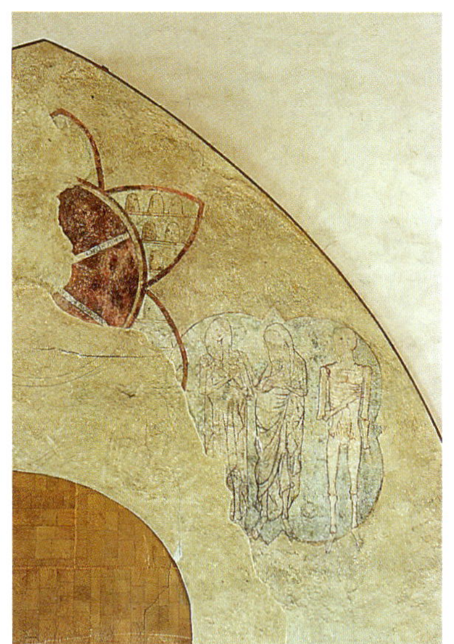

Fragments of stained glass found by E. Corroyer in 1875.

A THOUSAND YEARS OF BUILDING WORK

The Mont-Saint-Michel around 1390. Miniature from the "Très Riches Heures du duc de Berry".

The first constructions

A historico-liturgical text which appears to have been first written in the middle of the IXth century, gives us the oldest version of the foundation of the first oratory on the Mount in 708. We read that the position which the Archangel desired for the sanctuary was marked by a circular space, on which the morning dew did not settle, and in the centre of which rose two large rocks, which had to be cut away to level the ground. These legendary details can be the subject of an archaeological interpretation: we could in fact see in this two vertical slabs of an ancient ruined dolmen, with, around them, the trace of the mound which originally enveloped it. The hypothesis that there existed on the Mount a Neolithic monument, between the Vth and the IIIrd millennium is therefore perfectly plausible.

Constructions may also have existed on the rock during the Gallo-Roman period, at which time it was called Portis Herculis, the "Gate of Hercules". Some shards

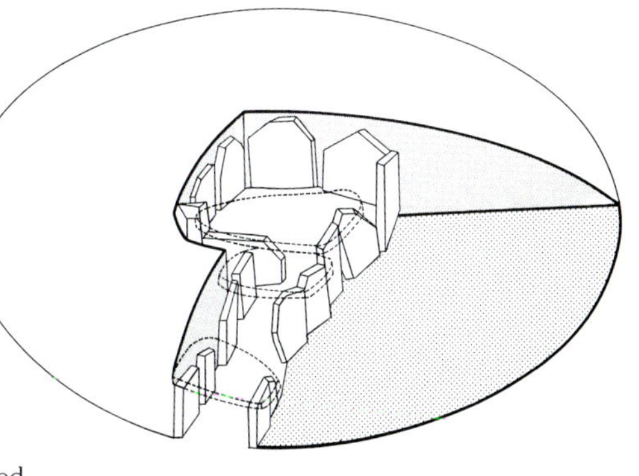

Section of a typical dolmen.

Behind the far wall of Notre-Dame-sous-Terre, an opening made in 1961 reveals a vestige of the oratory built by Saint Aubert in 708-709.

of mosaic discovered around 1880 suggest it, as does the mention in old chronicles of two oratories, built before 708 by anchorites and still visible in the XIIth century:

An oratory of the early middle ages built with bonded field-stone. Saint-Hermeland at Basse-Indre (Loire-Atlantique), a building dating from before 843. Here too the architecture evokes the idea of a cave.

the fact that these structures could be preserved for so long makes it impossible to regard them as basic hermits' shelters of the Merovingian period. It is more logical to view them as ancient Gallo-Roman edifices converted into sanctuaries at the time of the christianization of the bay, in accordance with an often-used procedure of reassignment (the chapel of Saint Agatha at Langon in Ille-et-Vilaine, for example).

But none of all that remains. We find the first traces of architecture on the Mount at the same time as we come out of the mists of unwritten history. The text mentioned above, "Revelatio Ecclesiae Sancti Michaelis" ("Revelation of the Church of Saint Michael) give a few indications on the construction and appearance of the first sanctuary. In 708, Archbishop Aubert of Avranches, having been thrice granted a vision of Saint Michael, decided to build a chapel on a small platform west of the crest of the hill. "He put up a building which did not finish in a point at the top, but was rounded in the form of a crypt which could contain, it is believed, a hundred people..."

This artificial cave on a circular plan was intended as a copy of the cave of Mont-Gargan, in southern Italy, where the first appearance of Saint Michael in the west took place at the end of the Vth century.

But this little chapel, looked after by a college of twelve priests in charge, soon became insufficient in the face of the growing success of the Mount as a place of pilgrimage. New buildings were therefore decided on. A fairly large church was built at the summit (the foundations were found during excavations in the abbey church, and are marked on the floor by red lines). It comprised a rectangular nave oriented east-west, with the entrance in the middle of the south wall, extended on the east by a narrower chancel, as was frequently the habit with pre-Romanesque architecture.

Further down, on the west, a solidly-built chapel replaced Aubert's modest oratory. This lower sanctuary has been preserved: it is the chapel of Notre-Dame-sous-Terre, crouched below the terrace of the church. Built on a square plan, it has two parallel naves, separated by a thick wall pierced with two arcades, which end in two small chancels with barrel-vaulting. Above the chancels is a gallery which was probably used to expose the relics for the veneration of the faithful.

This chapel shows all the characteristics of Carolingian architecture, which grew out of Roman structural tradition: very solid masonry made up of rubble-stones sunk "in a bath of mortar", bare wall surfaces with no attempt at rhythm (the two windows of the south wall are not in line with the arches of the central wall), arches built with flat bricks.

This venerable monument has aroused considerable perplexity in the minds of archaeologists. Some of them have believed that the central wall was added

Right: a plan of these buildings.
In black: Notre-Dame-sous-Terre, in grey, the revealed foundations of the church above. The outer line is the outline of the present-day abbey church.

Above: model of the Carolingian constructions on the top of the Mount.

after the chapel had been built. It is not so: this wall, linked to that of the west façade by some common lines of courses, shows the same materials, the same method of working, the same guiding line as the rest of the masonry of the chapel. The division into two naves is thus in fact the original layout.

Some have also wondered about the age of Notre-Dame-sous-Terre, since the chronicles are uncommunicative on this point. The brick arches, especially in the side niches of the sanctuaries, are completely identical to those which were recently found in the Carolingian walls of the château of Mayenne, whose lime joints yielded charcoal which permitted a radiocarbon dating of the second half of the IXth century. In addition, the double structure of the chapel reproduces that of the very ancient chapel of Saint Michael on Mont-Dol (Notre-Dame-sous-Terre is, incidentally, built on the line which joins the Mont-Saint-Michel to Mont-Dol): this relationship reveals a Breton influence which fits in with the narrow space of time (867-933) during which the Mount was Breton. All these elements combine to give Notre-Dame-sous-Terre a date around 900 (except for the vaults which were added later, no doubt in 992).

Other sanctuaries probably existed on the rock, surrounded by the individual wooden cells of the monks, when in 996 the duke of Normandy, Richard I, decided to entrust the Mount to the rich and enterprising Benedictine order. The sons of Saint Benedict, who throughout Europe were the biggest promoters of architectural works, were from then on to mark the rock with their talent as builders.

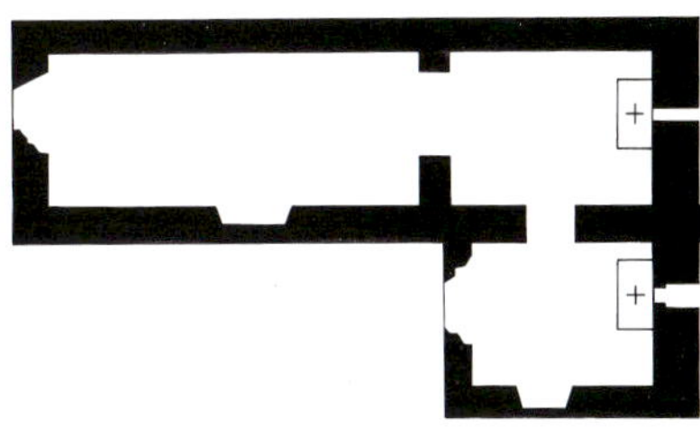

Plan of the Saint-Michel chapel of Mont-Dol. The double sanctuary went back to the early middle ages, the nave of the north sanctuary was more recent. This chapel was destroyed in 1802. (Departmental archives of Ille-et-Vilaine, 4 J.186).

Notre-Dame-sous-Terre, general view.

Niche in the north sanctuary of Notre-Dame-sous-Terre and Carolingian arches of the château de Mayenne (photo: Éditions Errance).

General view of the former ossuary. The masonry in the foreground dates from the XIIIth century, the square pier in the centre of the picture is XVIth-century. The structures in the background are Xth-century, modified in the lower part in the XVIth.

Former outer west wall, now within the Saint-Etienne chapel. Note the walled-up windows of the former side-aisle.

Below the monumental staircase of the Grand Degré, which rises from the entry of the abbey to the church, stretch the vaulted galleries which, from the XIth to the XVIth century, served the monks as a cemetery and ossuary. The attention of visitors is attracted by the large wheel of the windlass crane , put in place at the beginning of the XIXth century by the prison administration. This spectacular instrument eclipses the architecture of the building, which is in any case very inhospitable and complicated.

And in fact, the chronicle texts and an analysis of the masonry show a complex construction. The ossuary built by abbot Ranulphe de Bayeux (1055-1085) was put into disorder in the XIIth century when the Grand Degré was built under abbot Richard Turstin (1237-1264), then in the XVIth when abbot Guillaume de Lamps (1500-1511) installed the terrace of the Saut-Gautier.

However, an attentive examination of the walls enables one to see in these galleries the remains of an extremely interesting building dating from before the work carried out by abbot Ranulph. Without going into a very precise analysis of the masonry, which would occupy several pages of this book, we can reconstruct it thus:

It is a four-cornered building, built on the south flank of the rock, below the terrace which stretched on the south side the length of the Carolingian church built on the summit (see preceding pages). A single-storey building on very high bases, it reveals a plan of three naves of three bays oriented north-south. The central nave had a roof frame and was pierced by high windows while the side naves, which were lower, were roofed by continuous barrel vaults (the western one still exists, under the terrace of the Saut-Gautier) though they, too, had windows. The walls separating the nave were carried on rectangular piers which received without imposte Roman arches, with a single roll towards the central nave and a double roll on the other side. In the main nave, these piers were ornamented with a sort of flat buttress, weathered at the top, which had a purely decorative rôle: it did not reach high enough to contribute to the buttressing of the vaults of the side naves.

Apart from the piers and the keystones of the arches, which are made in a fine grey

From left to right: position of the original building within the section of the present-day buildings, reconstituted west exterior elevation and section. In grey: parts which still exist and can be seen.

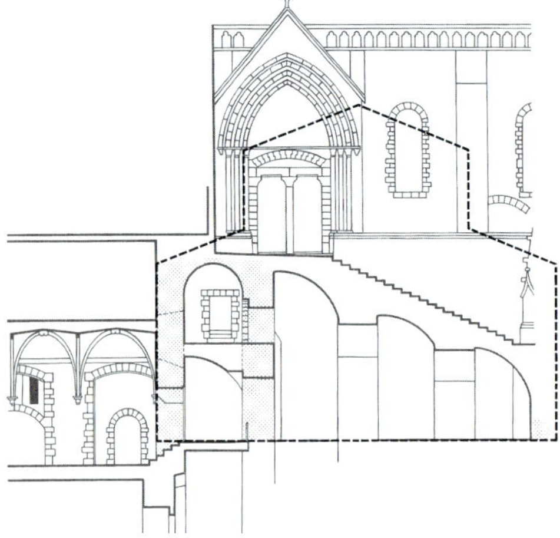

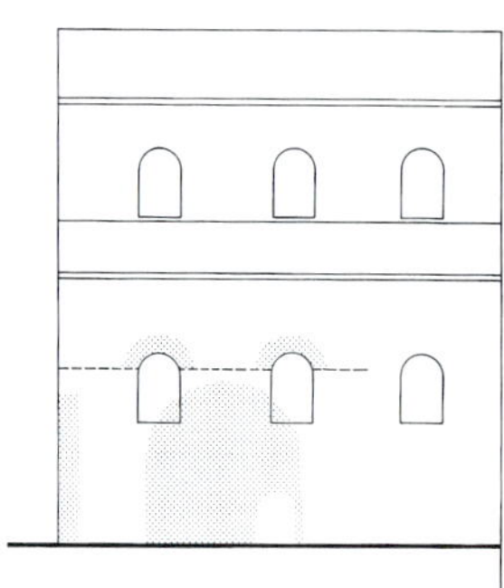

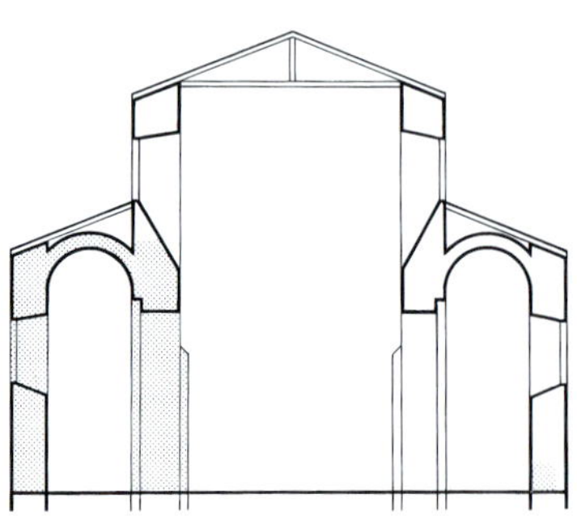

granite, all the masonry was made of rubble-stones extracted from the rock itself, roughly shaped with the pick and built up in regular courses, with here and there a flatter stone placed on edge or obliquely, as if the masons had wanted to make a sketchy attempt at an "opus spicatum" (herring-bone bond).

The building when thus reconstructed gives the impression of careful but archaic construction. The nature and the cut of the stones used are close to those of Notre-Dame-sous-Terre; the exterior walls have no buttresses. Stylistic analysis fully confirms this feeling. The windows, fairly broad and only slightly splayed, remind one of the way in which pre-Romanesque walls were pierced; the absence of a moulding at the spring of the arches does not allow the eye to discern a horizontal linking of the surfaces and helps to recall the severity of the walls in Carolingian edifices.

On top of this, the flat buttresses which ornament the square piers give an opportunity for comparison with buildings of known date. These buttresses exist in certain Romanesque churches with archaic architecture (Meusnes in the Loir-et-Cher, Calan in the Morbihan), but, above all, in the old cathedral of Alet, in Ille-et-Vilaine (second half of the Xth century) , where they mark the entry to the apse, and in the nave of the abbey church of Evron (Mayenne) which dates from the years 980-990, where they are placed in the same way as on the Mont-Saint-Michel.

All this comes together to date the building at the end of the Xth century, that is shortly after the arrival of the Benedictines on the rock. Now, the old chronicles establish that in 992, a fire ravaged the abbey, so that its buildings had to be rebuilt. This date is made even more plausible by the fact that that same year, the duke of Brittany, Conan I, killed at the battle of Conquereuil, was buried on the Mount in a Saint Martin chapel, which cannot be the crypt which currently bears that name, which was not built until after 1023. It would be difficult to imagine that the burial of this high personage in a chapel of the monastery should fail to be accompanied by a large donation, sure to have been invested in the rebuilding, finished in 996, of the parts which had been destroyed.

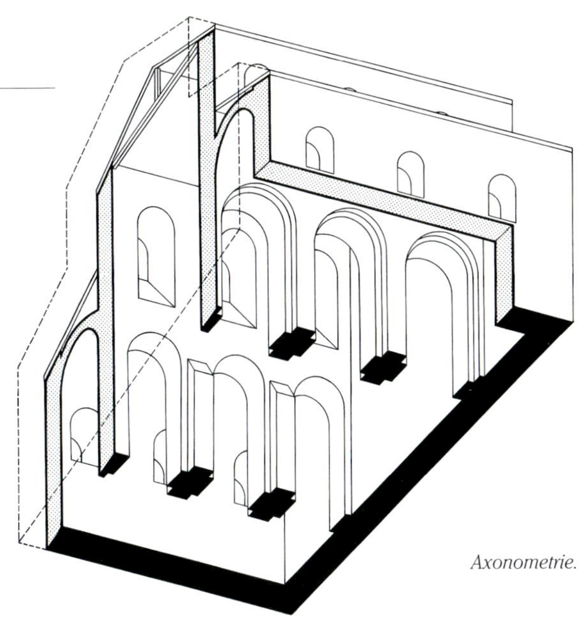

Axonometrie.

There is no reason that we should not believe that the building which we are reconstructing here, and which shows a shape very characteristic of a church with side-aisles, is this Saint Martin chapel the name of which was later transferred to the southern crypt of the abbey church: this zone south of the monastery was without the enclosure, and the large number of burials which are found there when work is being carried out show that it had a funerary function.

However this may be, this building of the extreme end of the Xth century shows us forms which are specific to a new architecture: stone vaults are put up, and space, rhythmically punctuated by technically unnecessary buttresses, is organized into well-defined bays, with the windows placed in line with the arches.

Thus we possess, within the old walls of the monks' ossuary, an exceptional and rare witness to the very beginnings of Romanesque art in western France.

Former cathedral of Alet, Ille-et-Vilaine (second half of Xth century).

Nave of Saint-Philbert-de-Grandlieu, Loire-Atlantique (Xth-XIth century).

Nave of Evron, Mayenne (around 980-990).

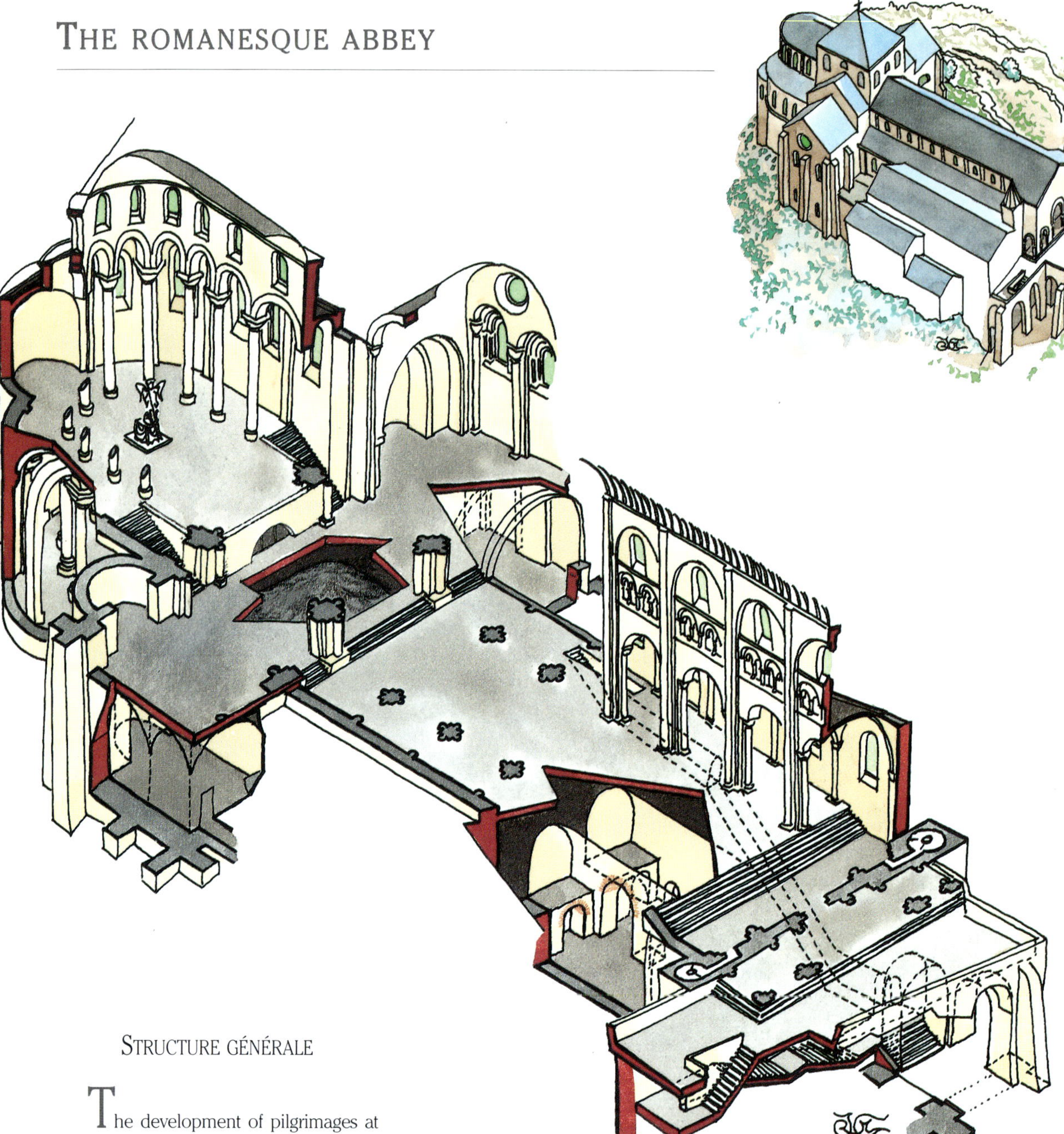

Aerial view and axonometric cut-away diagram of the Romanesque church with its foundation structures and original approach. Drawing by Robert-Henri Martin from information supplied by the author.

STRUCTURE GÉNÉRALE

The development of pilgrimages at the beginning of the XIth century, and the emblematic rôle of the Mount at the frontier between two rival but linked principalities (the duke of Normandy had just married the sister of the duke of Brittany, and the duke of Brittany had just married the sister of the duke of Normandy) together constituted the necessary conditions for putting in hand an important building project. It was therefore decided to build a new abbey church and new monastic buildings.

As was often the case the miraculous and opportune discovery of relics - in this case those of Saint Aubert - came only shortly before the granting of financial support. It is nothing more nor less than the preparatory putting-together of the dossier! So donations flow in, from the duchess Gonor, widow of Richard I, and above all from her son Richard II. This latter gave the abbey, among other things, the Chausey islands, from which was to be quarried the granite which, carried on barges as the tides allowed supplied the building site. The site was to be under way from 1023 to about 1080.

The project very ambitious from, the start: the church was to be built at the point of the hill, 80 metres [250 feet] above the sea-shore, and was to be 80 metres [250 feet] long. It was thus to be inscribed in a perfect square, symbol of the world created in its perfection and balance. Putting this proud project into effect called for some technical tours de force. The summit of the rock, as it turned out, makes available only a tiny area, and all that could be built there were the four pillars of the transept crossing, which bore the bell-tower and a small part of the nave. The rest of the church, the plan of which represented an immense cross, sat on an enormous foundation consisting of four crypts, placed at each of the four cardinal points, and which completely surrounded the point of the hill.

The ensemble formed a platform at the level of the summit, on which the abbey church was to be built. The general structure of this church was defined from the beginning, under the authority of the abbot Hildebert (1009-1023). It forms a gigantic staircase rising from west to east: in front of the terrace, there is a narthex before the western entrance, which opens on to a flight of steps leading to the nave, which is 1.5 metres (5 feet) higher. The nave extends in seven bays, with a central nave with a roof frame flanked by two vaulted side-naves. The transept, then, is again 50 centimetres [20"] higher. As to the Romanesque chancel, it is laid out as an apse surrounded by an ambulatory; it is 3 metres [10 feet] higher than the transept. The difference in level between the porch and the sanctuary is thus 5 metres [16 feet]; one can imagine how the pilgrims were impressed by this monumental organization of ascending volumes!

It has long been the custom to attribute the construction of this church to the Italian Benedictine Guillaume de Volpiano, abbot of Saint-Bénigné de Dijon and of Fécamp, and tireless reformer of the Norman abbeys. We now know that this great monastic figure of the year One Thousand had nothing to do with the design of the work. The politico-religious history of the abbey shows that the monks of the Mount, throughout the XIth century, fought with enormous energy against the centralism of Fécamp, which aimed at becoming the mother house of a federation under the authority of a single abbot. Guillaume de Volpiano, be it said, is not on the list of obituaries, the lists of monks of friendly houses for whom the monks were required to pray on the anniversary of their death: this omission is highly significant!

In reality, as we shall see as we analyze the oldest sections of the abbey church, the design of the monument is a reflection of the main characteristics of architectural creation in the time following close on the year One Thousand. We shall also see that although the project as a whole was conceived as from the years 1020-1025, the site was worked in several stages, each marked by varying influences and a different spirit.

THE EASTER CRYPT AND THE CHANCEL

The ancient historians of the abbey are unanimous in declaring that the construction of the church went from east to west. The construction thus started with the eastern crypt and the chancel which it carries. This latter collapsed in 1421, but the excavations carried out in 1908 and more importantly in 1964-65 permitted the rediscovery of the elements of its foundations and thus we can reconstruct its general layout.

It was composed of three straight bays ending on the east in a five-sided apse and was surrounded by an ambulatory. This, according to two miniatures which were made before 1421, was extended on the eastern side by an apsidiole. The crypt beneath was built on the same plan, though it had one straight bay fewer, on the eastern side, because of the slope of the rock.

Questions have since been asked about this type of plan with an ambulatory, of which we have here one of the earliest examples known in Normandy. It has been suggested that it is related, particularly, to the chancels of Jumièges and Fécamp and to the Romanesque cathedral of Rouen. This latter, the crypt of which was rediscovered during excavations, was built as from the year 990. It is true that it is built on a plan with an ambulatory, but with the addition of three radial chapels, each divided into three naves, and the vaulting of the crypt rests on pillars which are separate from the walls; none of these characteristics is present in the foundations of the chancel of the Mont-Saint-Michel. As to the

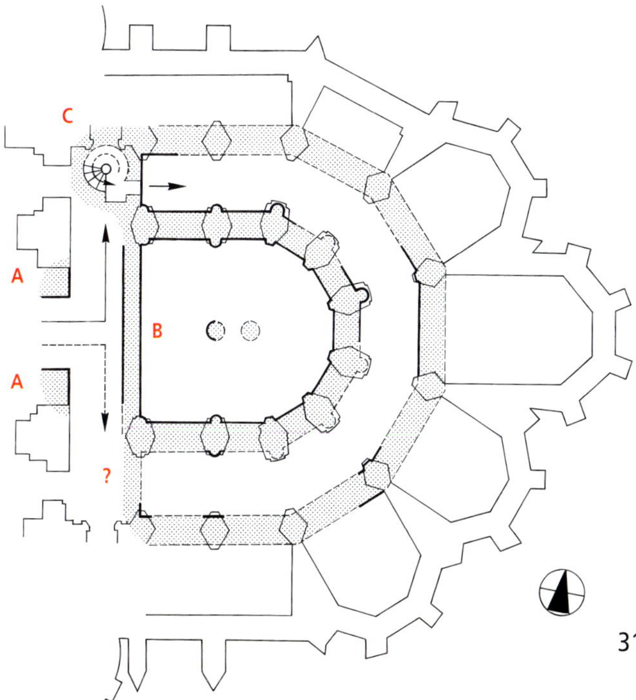

Summary of discoveries of elements of the east Romanesque crypt.

A and B: walls discovered in 1908 (wall B found once more in 1964-65).

Walls of the chancel and the ambulatory and central support found in 1964-65.

C: staircase discovered in 1991.

Fine continuous line: plan of flamboyant Gothic chancel.

Thick continuous line: Romanesque masonry actually observed.

Dotted line: reconstituted Romanesque masonry.

The arrows indicate the probable way down to the crypt from the crossing of the transept.

Two miniatures showing the whole of the Romanesque church: left, a very simplified version in "Li romanz del munt seint Michel" (XIVth century). Right, an accurate representation in the "Très Riches Heures du duc de Berry" (around 1390).

chancel of Jumièges, it has no crypt and building started as from 1040, more than 15 years after that of Mont-Saint-Michel. As to that of Fécamp, built around 990, we know only the meagre remains of a fragment of apse, and the ambulatory itself was built only at the end of the XIth century; besides which, we must remember that relations between Fécamp and Mont-Saint-Michel were at that time extremely strained (no mention of an abbot of Fécamp in the obituaries of the Mount during the whole of the XIth century). There is therefore no conclusive evidence allowing us to believe that the chancel of the Mount's abbey church derives from Norman models.

By contrast, the study of the relations of the Mount with other Benedictine abbeys, via the texts of the archives and comparative architecture, leads us in the direction of two other prestigious monasteries. The first is the abbey of Saint-Sauveur de Redon (Ille-et-Vilaine), which during the first years of the XIth had been under the authority of Mainard II, who was also abbot of Mont-Saint-Michel. His two successors in the seat of the abbot of Redon, Theudon and Cathwallon, are mentioned in the obituaries of the Mount: their reign coincides exactly with the time when the chancel of Mont-Saint-Michel was being built. The abbey of Redon has a chancel with an ambulatory, rebuilt in the XIIIth century but constructed, according to specialists, on Romanesque foundations. It is of very archaic shape, characterized by a widening towards the west, which would fit with a dating of about 1010 which the circumstances of the history of the monastery suggest. The arches of the nave also rest on embedded half-columns, as is the case of the crypt on the Mount..

The only remaining visible vestige of the crypt of the Romanesque chancel: spiral staircase (C on the plan on the preceding page).

The second is the abbey of Evron, in Mayenne, whose abbots, during the first decades of the XIth century, figured in the obituaries of the Mount. The excavations carried out there in 1985 brought to light the crypt of the Romanesque chancel, which has since disappeared. These remains, which are dated both by the texts and by radiocarbon as belonging to the years 980-990, enable us to reconstruct a raised chancel, surrounded by an ambulatory and with the addition of an apsidiole to the east, an arrangement identical with that at Mont-Saint-Michel. The hypothesis of an influence emanating from this region [which is now Mayenne and Sarthe - translator's note] is further strengthened by the comparison we made in the previous chapter and by the common features presented by the chancel of Mont-Saint-Michel and that of the abbey of La Couture at Le Mans (raised chancel and ambulatory).

So it is in Breton and southern Norman regions than we must probably look for the origin of the Romanesque chancel of Mont-Saint-Michel. We know nothing about the interior arrangement of this chancel, except that it was lit by broad windows above the big arcades and in the ambulatory. We can imagine that it was vaulted in stone, since it appears inconceivable that they would have built vaults on the transepts and not on the sanctuary.

The remains of the crypt that have been found allow us to make certain remarks and also to ask some questions. It was divided into two parallel naves by two central pillars, as in the present crypt; its vaulting rested on half-columns and pilasters embedded in the masonry. This detailed arrangement, which is absent in the other foundations of the church, shows that the crypt of the chancel had been the subject of a particularly refined architectural treatment. This is further confirmed by the particular layout of the link between the Romanesque chancel and the transept. We have seen that the chancel was elevated by 3 metres [10 feet]; it was no doubt reached by steps situated in the ambulatory, because between the two eastern pillars of the crossing of the transept there rose a vertical wall, pierced in the centre by large arched opening 3.5 metres [11 feet] in width. That was probably the monumental entry to the crypt from the upper church. An idea of the majestic character of such an arrangement is given by the beautiful Romanesque church of Saint-Hilaire in Poitiers.

Everything therefore suggests that the crypt of the chancel was considered as an especially important and sacred place in the monastery. Now, the Mont-Saint-Michel manuscripts which are today preserved at Avranches inform us that in the Romanesque crypt no ceremonies were performed, and that it was therefore not a place devoted to the cult. These contradictory data could be explained by a change of plan: in the first instance it was intended to make the crypt a reliquary chapel, perhaps there to lay the body of Saint Aubert which had been rediscovered a few years previously; later, this idea was abandoned, the rôle of reliquary probably passing to the chapel of Notre-Dame-sous-Terre, which it had been decided to preserve. This is fine example of those changes of mind which were so frequent in medieval building sites.

The North, West and South Foundations

The crypts which carry the two arms of the transept are still there. The northern one is known as Notre-Dame-des-Trente-Cierges (Our Lady of the Thirty Candles) (the monks lit thirty candles there during morning mass), the southern one is dedicated to Saint Martin. These two chapels are built on the same principle: a single square nave divided into two bays by a rib, a semi-circular apse with semidome vault to the east, framed by a series of interlocked arches which lead your eye towards the east window.

The atmospheres of the two are very different. The first, roofed with two groined vaults, shows an intimate, low, closed-in space; the rock, which has been left exposed in the south-west corner, evokes the feeling of a cave. A soft, comforting atmosphere therefore, appropriate to its dedication to the Virgin, "Mother of Mercy", and its function: Notre-Dame-des-Trente-Cierges was within the enclosure; the monks celebrated morning mass there at daybreak, and the office of Compline, the prelude to the silence of the night.

Saint Martin, by contrast, gives an impression of monumental power. Its vault is a continuous barrel-vault, on the east-west axis, of gigantic span (9 metres!) [30 feet!]. Its interior volume is contained in a cube; the apse opens as a perfect square topped by a pure semi-circle. These impressive and majestic shapes symbolize a ceremonial function. The Saint Martin crypt was without the enclosure (the manuscripts do not refer to any monastic ceremonies there) and opened on to a funerary zone at the foot of the south transept. It is probably in this

Crypt of Our Lady of the Thirty Candles.

Saint-Martin crypt.

Romanesque extension added on the west of the crypt of Notre-Dame-sous-Terre.

sanctuary, below the relics preserved in the southern arm of the church, that the high personages who were benefactors of the abbey were buried.

On the west flank of the rock, the venerable chapel of Notre-Dame-sous-Terre is preserved and encompassed in thick masonry. The north wall is reinforced, the south wall is lined with a very broad wall with a narrow barrel-vaulted corridor between the two; to the west the chapel is extended into a sort of vestibule, whose purpose is to support the western bay of the nave. Finally, the central pillar is thickened to bear in greater safety one of the piers of the upper church.

All the construction of these north, south and west foundations is very homogeneous. The walls are built in a large, regular bond, chequered by wide projecting grouted joints smoothed with an iron tool. The space is given animation only by the interplay of the massive ribs supported by sturdy pilasters, and the only decoration is a bevelled impost. It is all very severe and mural and not unreminiscent of the austere and monumental bareness of the Carolingian buildings.

Here again, the general atmosphere reminds one of the great abbey churches of Maine (Evron, or on the fringes of Angevin country, Château-Gontier) and Brittany (Locmaria de Quimper and, in the county of Rennes, the great rival of Redon, Saint-Melaine de Rennes, the oldest parts of which can, on analysis, be attributed to the first half of the XIth century). No doubt one can see here the hand of abbot Aumode (1028-1032), whose family, which originated in Le Mans, cultivated close links with Brittany. In the second half of the XIth century it was from this family that sprang abbot Almodius of Saint-Sauveur de Redon, who is mentioned in the obituaries of the Mount. And Aumode himself, who was close to the duke of Brittany, fell out of favour with Robert I of Normandy, who sent him away to die at Cerisy-la-Forêt.

THE TRANSEPT

We move into another world when we climb to the level of the high church. The northern arm of the transept was shortened in the XIIIth century and its apse was taken down in the XVIIth and then rebuilt during the restorations. But the southern arm, restored to its original layout by the architect Paul Gout, allows us to imagine the original splendour of the transept. Each of the two arms is made up of a square nave (with the exception of the north wall, which is definitely oblique) on to which opens an apsidiole with semidome vault surrounded with interlocking Roman arches. Animation is given to the gables and the west walls by powerful relieving arches, borne by embedded columns, and beneath which are large windows decorated with twisted mouldings and small columns. There is also an immense bulls-eye window in the upper part of the southern gable. Each arm is roofed with a north-south oriented barrel vault, the gigantic height and span of which are evidence of exceptional daring for the age (see the technical analysis of vaulting on page 21).

The whole ensemble is very full of light and monumental. The richness of the ornamentation and animation of the surfaces is in strong contrast with the sober severity of the foundation level. The particular accent of the studied architecture of this transept speaks of a new set of references. These, it seems, must be sought in one of the key sites of the epoch, the porch-tower dating from the years 1020-1035 of the abbey church of Saint-Benoît-sur-Loire, near Orléans, the work of the abbot Gauzlin, a bastard of Hugues Capet and half-brother of the king Robert the Pious. Gauzlin had conceived his tower as "an example for all Gaul". There we find exterior relieving arches, as in the west

Contemporary with the foundation buildings and the transept of the abbey church of Mont-Saint-Michel, the church of Bernay (second quarter of the XIth century) shows the experimentation of the first Norman Romanesque architecture, very different from what was then being built at Mont-Saint-Michel. The comparison shows clearly the originality and mastery of the architecture of the abbey church on the Mount.

The south arm of the transept.

wall of the southern arm of the Mount's abbey church, interlocked arches around the apsidioles, small columns and arches with mouldings framing the windows. The transept of Mont-Saint-Michel also shows elegant limestone capitals, with Corinthian decoration mixed with lions affrontee and fantastic birds, very like those of Saint-Benoît-sur-Loire.

This kinship with a prestigious *avant-garde* building reveals the authority of an art-loving abbot, with knowledge of the most advanced developments and trends in the architecture of his time, and open to other horizons than just those of western France. Only one name fits the part, Suppo, abbot of Mont-Saint-Michel from 1033 to 1048. This Italian monk, formerly abbot of Fruttuaria in Lombardy, was an intellectual and lover of grandeur, who considerably enriched the abbey's treasures and its library. It is probably to his influence that we owe the setting up in the Avranches area around 1040 of a very high-level school, to which fame was given by, among others, Lanfranc and Saint Anselme.

Limestone capitals in the transept.

Suppo's successor, Raoul de Beaumont (abbot from 1048 to 1053) was, according to the ancient historians of the abbey, the builder of the large pillars in the crossing of the transept. We do not know the original form of the crown above these pillars. It may have been a lantern-tower.

THE NAVE

The building of the church continues in the second half of the XIth century, with, once again, a marked change of accent. We are in the vigorous reign of William the Conqueror (1035-1087) and the new constructions will show a more markedly Norman character. The nave is entirely due to abbot Ranulphe (or Renoul) of Bayeux, formerly a monk at the abbey. It was divided into seven identical bays (of which only four still exist today), separated by embedded half-columns rising in a single bound from the floor to the top of the wall. Each bay is divided into three

General view of the south side of the church. A sharp change of emphasis: the transept shows a desire for fullness of space, the nave shows a desire to underline the composition of the structure.

levels, separated by horizontal mouldings. From the bottom upwards, the large arcades with double roll give on to lateral naves, then a clerestory, made up of two arcatures subdivided by a small column, opens on the roof-space of the side-aisles; finally, at the very top, there are huge high windows. Above these, a round relieving arch crowns each bay. This beautiful nave has a panelled roof-frame, while the side-aisles have groined vaults in each of the bays, which are separated by ribs.

The nave of Mont-Saint-Michel is cousin to the great Norman abbey churches of the second half of the XIth century. The embedded half-columns separating the bays can be found at Cerisy-la-Forêt, at Notre-Dame-sur-l'Eau in Domfront, at Montvilliers... The elevation on three levels is also widespread in William's Normandy. But unlike the naves of Saint-Etienne de Caen and Cerisy, where the intermediate level, which is as high as the large arcades, forms a real gallery, the nave of Mont-Saint-Michel is more closely related to those of Lessay, Saint-Nicolas de Caen and Boscherville, in which the arcades occupy half the height, and where the central level, of modest height, is only an element giving animation to the wall surfaces.

South side of the nave. The north side was rebuilt at the beginning of the XIIth century. (note the pointed arches in the side-aisle).

However, the nave of the abbey church on the Mount differs from contemporary Norman constructions in certain ways. First of all, there is no passageway pierced in the walls at the level of the high windows (an almost automatic arrangement in the biggest Romanesque churches of the duchy, with the exception of Jumièges and Saint-Nicolas de Caen). But above all, the presence of relieving arches above the high windows is a completely original arrangement. We know of no precedent for it, and no other example of this system exists in Normandy; the only relatively nearby church which seems to have been influenced by the Mont-Saint-Michel arches is a little Breton chapel, Sainte-Brigitte-de-Perguet, at Bénodet, in Finistère.

The technical function of this arrangement has often been over-estimated. It is certainly true that it can help to reinforce the stability of the pillars, by concentrating the weight of the roof, so that they can better resist the thrust of the groined vaults of the side-aisles. But the real interest of these arches is elsewhere. Their rôle is above all visual, and they help to give each bay its individuality by closing it back on itself. We are therefore dealing with a very different spirit from that of the major trends of Norman Romanesque architecture, where the continuity of volumes is generally clearly stated.

All in all, the nave of Mont-Saint-Michel thus appears as a work conceived in parallel with the main movement of Norman creativity, but powerfully original, without antecedents or posterity.

In 1103, the north wall, which had been finished some twenty years before, collapsed on to the building which had been built up against it on the north. This catastrophe was probably due to incomplete drying of the mortar, which was made with sea-sand containing a large amount of salt. According to some of the old historians of the abbey, reconstruction was not started, by the abbot Bernard du Bec (1131-1149), until thirty years later. It is

The abbey church of Jumièges shows a relationship with the nave of Mont-Saint-Michel.

Granite capital in the north side-aisle: the great whore of the Apocalypse riding on her beast.

impossible to believe that they waited so long to carry out this restoration; simple common sense forces us to date it in the years following 1103. The mention of the work carried out by abbot Bernard must in reality refer to repairs following a serious fire which happened in 1138.

In the reconstruction of this north wall, the main outline of the original approach was respected, but with noticeable differences showing a seeking after greater solidity. The clerestory of the intermediary level is less widely open and the arches of the side-aisle are pointed. The bays are no longer topped with a relieving arch. But above all, the masonry of the arcades is entirely bonded, and no longer formed of mortared rubble between two outer leaves. By contrast with the architect of the south wall, he who built the north was trying to make a rigid structure that could not be deformed and would bear the weight of the roof evenly throughout its fabric. The result is naturally less daring and elegant.

All the western part of the nave disappeared as a result of the fire of 1776. Before that it had been subjected to far-reaching modification, especially in the XIIth century (see below). Its original layout has however been known since the fruitful excavations of 1962-63. The XIth-century façade was preceded by a narthex of one bay, made up on the western side of a large arcade flanked on each side by a smaller one; two symmetrical arcades also opened on the north and south. The arches and vaults sprang from half-columns embedded in large piers.

Here again, we can compare the west front of the church with contemporary Norman constructions. A similar arrangement originally existed beneath the façade of the abbey church of La Trinité de Caen. We can get some idea of what it was like by looking at the narthex of the church of Saint-Nicolas in the same town. There is a difference, however, by comparison with the Caen buildings: the porch of the Mont-Saint-Michel abbey church had to support a wall which was very much open to the light from the west. In fact, fragments of stained-glass windows which can be dated to the period 1140-1150, found last century among the hardcore of the terrace, show that a window depicting the Passion could be seen on that side. We must therefor imagine, above the narthex, one or more windows of large dimensions, since a windows of the Passion requires a considerable surface.

THE PILGRIMS' CIRCUIT

The Romanesque church of the Mont-Saint-Michel was designed to receive crowds of pilgrims. Its designers were therefore faced with the problem of controlling the movement of very large groups. In the present state of our knowledge, only one hypothesis allows us to reconstitute the path followed by the faithful to the sanctuary and their access to the exit.

The present entrance to the abbey opens on the east, on to the external Grand Degré which is a continuation of the main street of the village. But originally the entrance was on the west: the pilgrims, when they had climbed the main street, made their way along the south face of the monastery and arrived at a monumental porch, pierced by large

Influence of the Mont-Saint-Michel nave: Sainte-Brigitte-de-Perguet at Bénodet (Finistère).

Narthex of Saint-Nicolas in Caen.

The great gallery rising from south to north, under the west terrace, led the pilgrims from the entrance to the square in front of the church. Two monumental doors on the right were no doubt to enable the faithful to enter and leave Notre-Dame-sous-Terre without having a file of people going in both directions.

arcades, which occupied all the western side of the walls. From there, they entered the enclosure and reached a majestic gallery with a barrel vault rising from south to north (it still exists under the terrace of the church) which they climbed to the next level. There, the staircase was continued by a parallel return flight the entrance to which, now walled up, can still be clearly seen in the masonry. One thus came directly from the porch to the square in front of the big doors of the high church.

The narthex then constituted a preparatory stage. It could also, as at Cluny, house the pilgrims when the church was completely filled by liturgical processions. The faithful then had to cross - a highly symbolic path - the seven bays of the central nave to arrive at last at the altar of Saint-Michel-en-la-Nef (Saint Michael in the Nave) (the transept and the chancel, reserved for the monks, were part of the enclosure), the final goal of their long journey. To avoid interfering with the flow which moved from the entrance to the altar, the exit was probably via the secondary staircase which starts in the high part of the nave and passes under the southern side-aisle to reach the west porch of the monastery at the level of the foundation buildings.

One last thing should be noted here: the pilgrims' upward journey was certainly interrupted by a ritual halt in the chapel of Notre-Dame-sous-Terre, a sacred spot revealed to Saint Aubert by the Archangel and where, according to several clues, the founder's relics were venerated. This progression towards the upper church, taking in a halt in an underground chapel dedicated to the Virgin, is not unlike the circuit of the pilgrims of the year One Thousand in the Pyrenean abbey of Saint-Michel-de-Cuxa, This coincidence could lend support to the idea that this whole route climbing from west to east, uninterrupted from the entrance of the monastery to the final point of the high nave, was clearly defined from the conception of the site at the beginning of the XIth century.

The Romanesque entrance.

Aerial view from the north-west and localization of the buildings of the Romanesque monastery.

THE MONASTERY. 1023-1149

Although the high architectural quality of the church and its foundation buildings allows precise analyses to be made, the same is not true of the Romanesque monastic buildings which surround the nave of the abbey church on three sides. These, in fact, were built from the very start with less care and fewer means. The walls, in particular, present too modest a thickness for buildings of several storeys, subject in addition to the enormous thrust of the vaults on the lower floors. They are built in an economical masonry in which the presence of small-calibre rubble-stones shows the use of materials retrieved from the demolition of buildings dating from before 1023.

The fragility which is the result of the mediocrity of building techniques has made these buildings vulnerable to accidents of all sorts: monstrous hurricane in 1117, earthquake in 1155, fires in 1112,1138, 1204, 1300, 1350, 1374, etc. It is therefore no surprise to find replaced, repaired, seamed masonry, the analysis of which is made even more difficult by traces of modifications made for the sake of enlargement or change of use.

Let us therefore restrict our description of these parts to the broad outlines. The main body of the Romanesque monastery, the building of which, according to the chroniclers, is due to abbot Ranulphe, is a long building built to the north, facing the sea, along the whole length of the nave of the church. It contains three levels, the first two with stone vaulting. On the ground floor, the hall of the Aquilon is the old Romanesque almonry, which originally opened on the western porch of the abbey. The second floor houses the length of the Promenoir (covered walk). This curious name is not very old: the chroniclers of the XVIIth century use it but we cannot establish which hall they meant by it, and it was only in 1853

Dormitory.

Hall of the Promenoir, Romanesque refectory and chapter hall.

Hall of the Aquilon. Romanesque almonry.

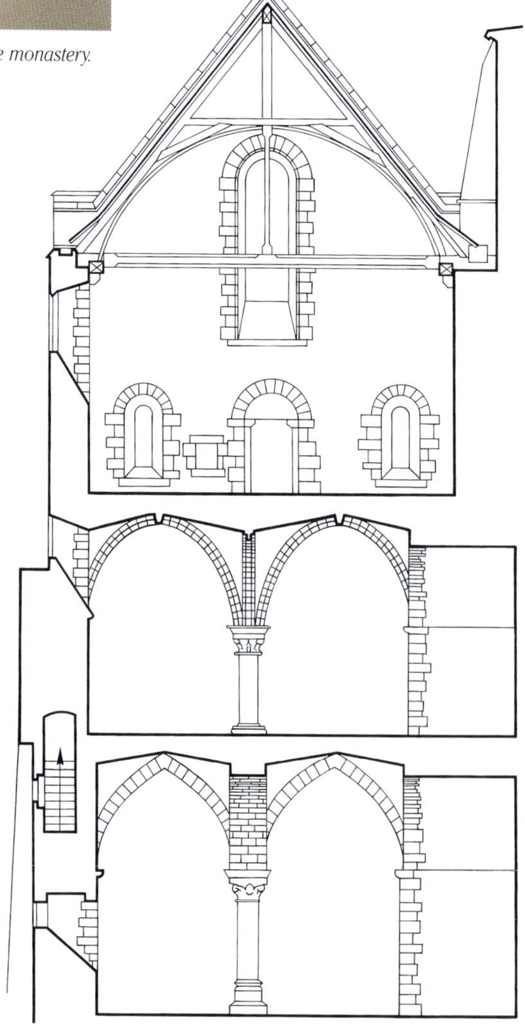

Capitals in the Promenoir.

Hall of the Promenoir.

that the historian Maximilien Raoul gave this name to the middle floor of the Romanesque abbey. Recent research has enabled us to define the true function of this room, which served both as refectory and as chapter-hall (and perhaps as scriptorium). Above, on a level with the church and communicating with it, is the dormitory, which has a vaulted roof-frame.

To the north of this building, subsidiary buildings, some of which have disappeared, housed secondary elements, in particular an infirmary on the level of the dormitory and a kitchen on the level of the Promenoir

To the west, part of the west porch, which was built at the same time as the foundation buildings of the church, was walled in during the second half of the XIth century. In the upper part of the space thus cut off, two small barrel-vaulted chambers were built. It is usual to regard these as having been used for the management of the abbey's secular seigniorial interests. Their position, near the entrance and outside the enclosure, makes this identification very believable.

Finally, to the south, the chapel of the year One Thousand, described in the previous chapter, was disused and transformed into an ossuary, opening via a large arcade on to the platform used as a cemetery which stretches between this building and the Saint-Martin crypt.

Let us also note that a cloister existed in the Romanesque abbey. The texts have nothing to say about where it was situated, but we may imagine that it occupied the position of the small courtyard squeezed between the dormitory and the northern arm of the transept; that is in fact the only possible location, with respect to the available space and to the functional interdependence of the various functions of the monastic institution. Originally built in wood, it was rebuilt in stone by abbot

Hall of the Aquilon.

Beneath the west terrace, a pretty Romanesque hall which has recently been rediscovered. It has been given the name of "the Hall of the Fleurs-de-Lys", because of its painted decoration (XIIIth century). It was created in the second half of the XIth century by creating an entresol in one of the arcades of the Romanesque porch, the walled-in arch of which can be seen on the right.

Roger II (1106-1123). Remains of the fixture of a lean-to roof in the little courtyard could be evidence of this minute cloister.

In the XIIth century work goes on under abbot Roger II. It is to this abbot that we owe a number of repairs and constructions: the vaults of the Romanesque monastery rebuilt after the collapse of the north wall of the nave in 1103, and above all the building of a huge ensemble on the north flank of the rock. We know nothing of this new building, which occupied that present position of La Merveille, apart from the fact that it was made up of two bodies aligned east-west, and that it contained an upper floor with vaulted roof-frame above a vaulted ground floor. Part of the walls of La Merveille, up to first-floor level, are remains of this structure, and the main structure of Almonry is very probably a hall built by Roger II.

This whole ensemble was riddled with narrow vaulted tunnels, hollowed out of the thickness of the walls, which made their way along all the constructions of the north flank, then turned to rejoin the western halls. The "secret" passages, of which a few stretches remain, may have had a defensive rôle (spy hole in the hall of the Aquilon), but their principal use must have been to enable the monks to move about from one part of the abbey to another when the halls were occupied by the numerous members of the suites of attendants brought by great personages who had come on pilgrimage.

A last phase of works is attested to in the first half of the XIIth century, under the authority of abbot Bertrand de Bec. This intellectual monk, trained in the antique ways of thought in the great schools of Paris, had the crossing of the transept roofed with a spreading ogival vault supporting a square tower with cut-off corners ornamented with columns. He also had stained-glass windows made in the church, in particular a large depiction of the Passion, close in style to the prestigious achievements of the cathedrals of Le Mans and Chartres.

THE CONSTRUCTIONS OF ABBOT ROBERT

The second half of the XIIth century saw the beginning of new phases of construction. The abbot at the time was Robert de Thorigny (1154-1186), a figure who has today become emblematic and whose political and intellectual rôle has been tolerably well exaggerated. This skillful courtier of king Henry II of England was above all an efficient administrator and was quickly able to refloat the parlous finances of the monastery.

Robert de Thorigny started by making a considerable modification to the silhouette of the church by replacing the covered porch with a façade with two towers. This idea was in the air at the time. In 1145 abbot Robert had seen the façade of Chartres being built, and perhaps that of Saint-Denis, which had been built five years earlier. We also know that a little later he had seen the works going on at Notre-Dame de Paris. At the same time, abbot Pierre de Celle (1162-1181), who was head of the Saint-Remi monastery at Reims, carried out the same transformation... One of the towers, which contained Robert's personal library, collapsed some while later; the other was demolished after the 1776 fire. Their silhouette, according to the illustrated documents, was bare and severe, the only animation being given by rare openings and buttresses without projections at the corners.

To the west, Robert de Thorigny enlarged the square by building a new projecting block. This contained three levels. Beneath the terrace, two chambers with pointed barrel vaulting made up his personal lodging; on the lower level stretched a hall, also vaulted, which must have served as porters' lodge and guardroom for the protection of the western porch. Beneath

The south tower around 1690.

Robert de Thorigny's bedroom. The windows face west, and look out on the incomparable spectacle of sunset over the bay.

this again, at the deepest level of the foundation buildings, the dungeons were hollowed out, the "Twins", to which the only access was a trapdoor let into the vaulting. These sinister holes remind us that the abbot, although he was the father of his monks, was also a lord of high justice!

The south tower around 1390.

Finally, to the south, Robert set up a series of constructions between the ossuary and the western porch. The bulk of it is a huge building on the southwest corner of the monastery. It contains, above a floor of deep cellars, a large hall with a pointed barrel vault which is usually called the "Guest house", although the old texts have nothing to say about the use it was intended for. The fact that it communicates with the Romanesque porch makes this interpretation by Paul Gout very believable. Above this hall there was a floor with a roof-frame whose use is unknown. It may have been a place devoted to the administration of the abbey since it communicated directly with the Romanesque halls already used for that purpose and also with the abbot's lodging.

Between this building and the ossuary, it is again to abbot Robert that we owe a building on two levels containing, from bottom to top, a small vaulted hall and the present chapel of Saint-Etienne. There again we have no information on the original purpose of this building; we can only suppose that it had a funerary function in view of its direct link with the ossuary.

It is today very difficult to interpret the whole of this ensemble. The south-west building collapsed in 1818, and the chapel of Saint-Etienne was subsequently deeply modified. A consideration of these structures nevertheless allows us to imagine the overall silhouette of the abbey as pilgrims of the end of the XIIth century must have found it: an enormous church of contrasting masses, to which animation was given by the façade towers, the impressive bell-tower and the raised chancel, and below it, like a gigantic rampart, an uninterrupted series of buildings covering the northern flank of the rock, the western flank and the southern flank for the whole length of the great nave.

At the very end of the XIth century and the beginning of the XIIth both technical innovations and a renewal of mystical thought blossomed under the influence, in particular, of great Benedictine figures like Suger, abbot of Saint-Denis. This creative ferment gave rise to the invention of a new architecture, called "French" in the texts of the time, and later "Gothic" (with a hint of disdain) as from the XVIth century. The first work of this new school, nothing more nor less than a manifesto, was the chancel of the abbey church of Saint-Denis, built by Suger and consecrated in 1144.

The vaulting of the Promenoir.

The abbey of Mont-Saint-Michel, in the long history of its constructions, shows all the signs of the revival of interest which heralded the birth of this new architecture. The Romanesque church itself already vaguely foreshadows the basic ideas of Gothic techniques and thought. As we have seen (page 21), the architect of the 1023 church, by superimposing the Saint-Martin crypt and the southern arm of the transept, had thought up a sophisticated system of localization of weight and buttressing of thrust. As to the architect of the nave, he had designed a nave which was conceived, not as a continuous volume, but as a succession of sequences - the bays - which were strongly individualized and repeated in identical fashion: each of them, in elevation, foreshadowed that of the first-generation Gothic cathedrals (Chartres, for example). Finally, the façade with two towers counted among the first attempts which were to end up as the great harmonic compositions such as that of Notre-Dame de Paris.

Leading up to intersecting ribs.
Top: north tower of Bayeux cathedral.
Bottom: Lessay church.

In 1103, the north wall of the nave, which had been finished twenty years previously, collapsed on to the building which was up against it, the vaults of which were split and dislocated. Its reconstruction was to allow the use of quite new techniques. In the side-aisle and the hall of the Aquilon, the groined vaults are built up on bonded ribs shaped as pointed arches; this system had then been known for several years and was used, in particular, in the key site of Cluny (Cluny III, begun in 1088).

But above all, the hall known as the Promenoir, on the first floor, shows us vaulting on intersecting ribs which counts among the first such known. We can put it to the account of abbot Roger II, who was invested with the dignity of abbot in 1106; the chronicles attribute to him the reconstruction of the building and its stone vaulting.

So the vaults of the Promenoir follow very closely after the prototypes which illustrate the history of intersecting ribs: around 1070, large flat ribs were bent across the underside of the north tower of the cathedral of Bayeux; a few years later, real intersecting ribs were put up in the abbey church of Lessay (Manche, before 1098) and in that of Durham (England, after 1093).

The intersecting ribs of the hall of the Promenoir, which are very crude, show evidence of clumsy trial and error, blemished by technical errors. The ribs are made up of very short arch-stones separated by thick joints; thus there is a multiplicity of compressible elements which give a high degree of elasticity to the arches; thus the ribs give no rigidity and are subject to considerable deformation under the thrust of the masonry. The springs fall on the walls haphazardly, sometimes on openings in the wall...

The whole thing, however, stays up thanks to two things: the continuing goodwill of the Archangel, and also, and above all, the thickness of the vault, which ensures its cohesion through the mass effect of the mortar. So we are still dealing with Romanesque vaults, but they are evidence of the attention paid by the Mount's architects to the new techniques: in the XIIth century, minds are prepared so that the shapes of the new architecture shall will soon blossom forth into marvellous constructions.

Astonishing fall of the springs on an opening in the wall!

Cut-away diagram of La Merveille interpreted in curved perspective. Drawing by Robert-Henri Martin.

Aerial view from the north-west and position of La Merveille.

LA MERVEILLE
GENERALE STRUCTURE

April 22nd (an important date in the history of authoritarian powers: foundation stone of the Bastille, birth of Lenin...) of the year 1204: the Breton troops of king Philippe Auguste - busily conquering Normandy in the course of a lightning war - were ready to go into action before Mont-Saint-Michel. The besieged rock offered resistance, aided by the tides, which forced the Bretons to withdraw. But they did not leave without having set fire to the village, and the conflagration, helped by the wind, reached the abbey, which suffered considerable damage.

Abbot Jourdain (1191-1212), who was at the time at loggerheads with his monks, undertook only a few repairs. It was necessary to wait for the consecration of his successor, Raoul des Iles (1212-1228), before a really serious work of reconstruction was

The pretty little hall squeezed in between Our Lady of the Thirty Candles and the Promenoir is contemporary with the first plans for La Merveille. It was shut off when it was decided to enlarge the wing of the cloister. Its present-day romantic name, "Devil's dungeon" is recent. It was probably originally the hall of the "little chapter", which was used only for short evening ceremonies (readings before the last office and ritual hand-washing on Saturday).

put in hand. The fire had chiefly damaged the building put up a century earlier by abbot Roger II on the northern flank of the rock. The walls, however, had remained standing and could be re-used, as well, probably, as one of the halls of the ground floor (the present Almonry). It is on the basis of these remains that Raoul des Iles, thanks to a generous royal subsidy, was to have built a new monastery, in the Gothic style, which today we call La Merveille.

It seems that the first project was to retain the general structure of Roger II's building, while nevertheless enlarging it by adding a further storey: traces of restoration in the east wall of the west wing show that a layout with two naves had been intended on that side, no doubt identical with the previously-existing Romanesque edifice. But this idea was soon abandoned in favour of a much more ambitious project, which recent studies have made it possible to define. The general conception was a very proud one. It was intended to add an additional wing to the west and thus to form an ensemble of three buildings, on an east-west alignment, each of which would have three levels. The project thus incorporated the vertical interpretation of an important figure in Christian symbolism, the square divided into nine boxes (3 x 3). This geometric outline, which gives rise to the plan of major monuments like the porch-tower of Saint-Benoît-sur-Loire, is the reference grid representing the celestial Jerusalem as it is described to us by the book of Revelation: a square city each face of which is pierced by three gates.

The idea is therefore on a very lofty spiritual plane. It is also on a very lofty intellectual plane: each of the three buildings planned is organized on a symbolic theme like chapters in a book. This very rigorous disposition (each building had to show the same structure: three levels and seven bays) is evidence of the influence of the universities, which were being created at that time in towns with which Mont-Saint-Michel enjoyed close relations: several abbots had been learned men, educated in the greatest schools, especially Paris.

The eastern building, the first to be built, contained from bottom to top the Almonry, where the pilgrims were welcomed, the Guest Hall, where visitors of high rank feasted, and the monks' refectory. This superpositioning represented the hierarchy of medieval society, formalized in the XIth century: "those who work, those who fight, and those who pray" (third estate, nobility, clergy).

The next building contained on the ground floor the food and drink store, then the monks' work-room or scriptorium,. and at the top the cloister, a place of prayer and meditation. Thus material, intellectual and spiritual nourishment were superposed.

Finally, the western building, was to contain at the bottom a court-room, symbolizing Justice, considered in the middle ages as the most important of the four cardinal virtues; on the first floor a new infirmary was to represent Charity, first of the three theological virtues; on the second floor, a chapter hall was to signify Obedience, a fundamental monastic virtue

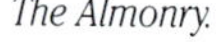

The Almonry.

The Guest Hall.

according to the Rule of Saint Benedict. Thus it was planned that the virtues should be distributed in the hierarchy of Benedictine perfection. This third building, as we shall see later, was never built.

THE ALMONRY AND THE GUEST HALL

The Almonry is divided into two naves roofed with simple groined vaults carried on a central row of six round columns topped with smooth capitals. As we have seen, it is probably a XIIth-century hall, witness to the building of Roger II.

Above is stretches the Guest Hall. Its entrance, on the south, is preceded by a porch, now walled up. On the same side, a pretty chapel, dedicated to Saint Magdalen, is built up against it: this oratory, roofed with two bays of ribbed vaulting, was no doubt reserved for the private devotions of visitors of mark. A wall hatch allowed them to follow the mass from the hall, while still remaining segregated from the faithful. This arrangement is very frequent in the domestic chapels of lordly dwellings.

The Guest Hall was separated into two naves by a row of slim columns. Two monumental fireplaces, in the west wall, constituted the kitchen section, separated from the rest of the room by a tapestry fixed to a transverse beam the supports of which are still visible: pilgrims of high rank, conforming to the habit of their class, ate meat, while the ordinary pilgrims, who were received on the ground floor, shared the frugal fare of the monks, who were forbidden by their Rule to eat four-legged animals. A third fireplace, which has now disappeared, was built in the centre of the south wall and heated the hall itself. Finally, an indispensable adjunct to a dining hall, latrines completed the equipment, suspended in corbelling between the outer buttresses.

All that corresponds to a very precise functional programme, as the specific organization of the space also indicates. The Guest Hall, which is one of the most beautiful volumes of the abbey, is in fact a princely hall. The painting, the coloured glass windows, the enamelled floor-tiles with the arms of France and of Castille, have disappeared, but the space, very open, has kept its splendid airiness: the eye can travel about it very freely, the slimness and spacing of the columns give perfect transparency. The internal buttresses and the relieving arches at each bay give a majestic rhythm to the side walls, which a multitude of vertical lines (columns thinned down as far as possible, narrow lancet windows, small columns on the buttresses) draw the eye upwards to the ideal lightness of the groined vaulting. The carved decoration also adds to this elegance: the capitals, long and narrow, are ornamented with leaves of a noble simplicity, carried on long stalks which follow the

Capitals in the Guest Hall.

line of the ribs of the vault. The carving, clinging closely to the surface of the bell, thus leads the eye towards the arches with no superfluous reliefs to hinder its flight.

The Guest Hall is thus a pure masterpiece of architecture, as much by the perfection of its shapes as by the technical mastery of its design (see page 23, analysis of the buttressing of the vaults). It forms part of a series of prestigious creations of which it is as it were the pivot. In fact it has inherited the researches carried out by the architects of the Plantagenet domain of the years 1180-1190: the great hospitallers' halls of Anger (Saint-Jean hospital) and Le Mans (maison-Dieu de Coeffort) already show us an open and transparent space, obtained by the spacing and extreme thinning of the columns, which reveals the audacious lightness of the groined vaulting.

Later, the great Ile-de-France abbeys of Saint Louis show us huge vaulted refectories with two naves whose relationship to the hall on the Mount is obvious. Royaumont and Saint-Martin-des-Champs, in "Paris, show that the king's architects transposed directly into the monastic architecture of the royal domain the design of the Guest Hall. This is, however, thoroughly Norman, as is attested by a number of constructional details (circular abaci of the capitals, for example). We must therefore consider is as a prototype, invented on the spot from regional experience and destined to found a superb posterity.

THE REFECTORY

Above stretches the monks' refectory. This upper storey, near the sky, expresses by its space and lighting the idea of divine unity. Nearly 50 metres [165 feet] above the rock, the logical choice of roofing this hall with a vaulted roof-frame (a stone vault would have necessitated buttressing which would have been very difficult to carry out), made it possible to dispense with a row of supports in the centre. Thus the monks' dining hall is a single immense nave with ample airiness. The rhythm of the volume, so marked on the floor below, is here completely dissipated; the rapidity with which the windows follow one another no longer gives a metre but a vibration. Finally, the light is diffused with incomparable softness and

The refectory seen from the west.

evenness, filtered by walls which are veritable screens.

The spirituality of the refectory is also expressed by the curious optical effect which strikes the visitor as he crosses the threshold. From the entry, the side walls seem solid, although light is streaming in. As the observer progresses further and further into the room, long narrow windows open up one after another, and then close again behind him. This visual effect is not meaningless: the eye first discovers a closed space, symbol of the enclosure, which is isolation with respect to the world, while at the same time light, the visible sign of the divine presence ("God is light", abbot Suger had written at the door of the abbey church of Saint-Denis), comes through the walls and fills the refectory.

But the place of earthly food was also the place of spiritual food. The Benedictine monks ate in silence and communicated only by a precise code of gestures. During the meal, the "duty" monk for the week officiated from the pulpit built in to the south wall, chanting "recto tono" pious and edifying texts. His voice, projected from wall to wall by the acoustic panels formed by the oblique embrasures of the windows, is amplified by the resonance chamber of the panelled roof-frame and can be clearly heard throughout the hall.

This very Benedictine atmosphere of spirituality, at once impressive and serene, is brought about by a technical device of extreme originality and cleverness. To lighten the upper part of the extremely high walls of the building, while still retaining the solidity necessitated by a roof-frame with an immense span and an extremely heavy roofing of schist, the architect replaced the side walls by a succession of piers stiffened by their lozenge-shaped section. The weight, thus divided among a multitude of small, rigid and non-deformable pillars, is thus supported without effort and without any weak point; at the same type, the approach adopted lighten the wall to the maximum extent thanks to the multiplicity of windows between the piers and their very open embrasures. In the last analysis, this technical conception is surprisingly modern: the idea boils down to replacing walls by stiffening members, and in a way foreshadows the basic principles of metallic architecture.

The reader's pulpit fits in without breaking the rhythm of the wall.

But here, the technical achievement is not the most important thing: it is put to the service of a programme of mystical spirituality, and this double nature, evidence of a double perfection, makes the refectory one of the absolute masterpieces of Gothic architecture.

The refectory seen from the east.

The amazing idea of the screen-wall shows the genius of the designer of the refectory.

Let us note, to conclude this examination of the eastern building of La Merveille, that a kitchen was built up against the refectory, on the south side, above the porch of the Guest Hall. It was replaced in the XVIIth century by a large staircase, but has nevertheless preserved one of its most interesting features: within the thickness of the walls between this kitchen and the refectory, a circular shaft descends as far as the ground floor. It is the shaft of a service-lift which allowed the pilgrims' meals to be sent directly to the Almonry, so that they thus shared the frugal diet of the monks.

THE FOOD AND DRINK STORE

The ground floor of the western building of La Merveille is occupied by the food and drink store, a vast, cool, dark hall where provisions were stored. Two rows of powerful square pillars, with no decoration other than an abacus, separate the space into three naves roofed with groined vaults. The northern one, as in the hall on the next floor, is reduced to the width of a simple corridor: this curious arrangement has the effect of shrinking the span of the vaulting and causing is to adopt a very acute angle; the resultant of the downward weight is thus brought back as far as possible from the vertical and to that extent relieves the outer wall from lateral thrust. A large opening towards the outsi-

The food and drink store.

The scriptorium.

de, on the same side, has retained traces of the fixing of a winch crane which was used to hoist the supplies.

The scriptorium

The first floor is known as the Hall of the Knights. This appellation goes back only to the XVIIth and XVIIIth centuries, at which time the hall was decorated with a panel bearing the names of the knights who had defended the Mount during the Hundred Years' War. Romantic literature has since muddled this up with the Knights of Saint Michael, a military order founded by Louis XI at the château of Amboise in 1469. In fact, this large room was within the enclosure (it does not communicate with the neighbouring Guest Hall), and was the monks' common room. There is a large measure of agreement today that it should be considered as the scriptorium (copying room) and library. This usage is almost certain, even if the room may have had other functions in parallel, especially that of warming room.

The Hall of the Knights occupied the central place in the great unfinished project of La Merveille. It therefore communicated directly with the other monastic facilities. In the north-east corner, a spiral staircase joined it to the refectory and the Almonry. On the north-west, another allowed one to go down to the food and drinks store, and a third, passing through the little building of the archivist, led to the cloister. In the east wall, a door opens on to a narrow round-arched passage, hollowed out within the thickness of the masonry, which led to the XIth- and XIIth-century monastery rooms. Finally, along the length of the south wall, a raised gallery, once separated by a dividing wall, gave direct access from the porch of the Guest Hall to a stairway which climbed to the church; no doubt this way was taken by the personages of high rank who had come on pilgrimage to the Mount, and who thus passed through the enclosure without entering it.

Since it was a monastic place, dedicated to silence and study, the Hall of the Knights shows us an atmosphere very different from that of the Guest Hall. Its inside space offers no springing verticality and no transparency. It is divided into four

Capitals in the scriptorium.

The scriptorium seen from the south gallery. The round windows contribute to the spirituality of the hall (see symbolic analysis of shapes, page 17).

naves separated by three rows of columns, the southern row bedded on the rock, the other two on the pillars of the food and drink store. These columns with thick, sturdy shafts, encumber the room by compartmentalizing it; you are left with the impression of a volume cut up into rationally delimited squares, as if we were looking at different work spaces for the monks.

Here, the eye is not carried up towards the vaulting. The capitals have a vegetable decoration (cabbage and lettuce leaves) which is heavy, thick and complicated. Above this, the abaci stick out a long way; their relief is still further accentuated by a scotia (a very deep concave moulding) cut out in their underside. This detail of moulding, which is typically Norman, has an essentially graphic rôle, and is there to catch and hold the shadow and make a black line, like a pencil line, whose purpose is to stop the eye in its upward movement: the monk's eye should not be lost in distant prospects!

A serene and studious atmosphere, therefore, but also charged with spirituality: the large circular bays pierced in the north wall symbolically represent the celestial world and are a reminder that the monks' work is inspired by heaven and must be dedicated to it.

The room is provided with two fireplaces built on the north side. This arrangement is not in keeping with the usual Benedictine habit (normally heating is restricted to the kitchen, the infirmary and the warming room). Here it is made necessary by the ambient dampness: the room faces north and west and above it is the open platform of the cloister. It was therefor absolutely necessary to maintain a dry atmosphere in order to ensure the preservation of the books.

Lastly, as in the other room on the first floor, latrines complete the equipment. Suspended in corbelling between the outer buttresses, they are reached via a sort of balcony, open on to the infinity of the bay through an elegant trefoiled clerestory.

THE CLOISTER

At the top of the western building of La Merveille, at the level of the abbey church, stretches the cloister. Suspended at 77 metres [252 feet] above the shoreline, it is the "Hortus Conclusus", the enclosed garden of the medieval mystics. Surrounded by covered galleries supported by delicate arcading, it offers an area of vegetation directly open to the sky.

We may imagine that there was originally a real garden, but it must have been done away with subsequently because of problems of infiltration, since it no longer existed at the beginning of the XVIIth century. It was reconstituted in 1623 and planted with box and flowers, but was once more done away with in 1676: the waterproofing techniques of the time - lead sheeting on the extrados of the vaults of the floor below - were neither very reliable nor long lasting. The present garden, made in 1965 using modern methods of waterproofing, was designed by father Bruno de Senneville, the founder of the present-day monastic community. Despite the unusual character of the distribution - vertical rather than horizontal - the cloister is, as in all monasteries, at the centre of the organization of the services. The refectory and kitchen open on to the eastern gallery, access to the church and the way down to the "Promenoir" and the crypt of Notre-Dame-des-Trente-Cierges, and the dormitory, all open on the south side.; in the eastern gallery, near the north-west corner, the adjoining archivist's building contains two small rooms one above the other, where the treasures and the archives were kept; it also contains a staircase leading directly to the Hall of the Knights on the floor below. Finally, the triple bay opening on to nothingness, on the same side, corresponds to the new Chapter-hall, which was never built.

By contrast with the church and the other parts of La Merveille, which present grandiose volume effects, the cloister is on a human scale: the dimensions of the human body give the height ands spacing of the small columns, and their progression is adjusted to a slow and meditative walk. This proportioning makes an intimate place of it, which is evidence of the Benedictine desire to ensure the full individual development of the monks. In fact, the monks pray, work, eat and sleep communally; the cloister is the only place where they can, for a few brief moments, enjoy the relaxation of personal freedom.

The galleries, roofed with a vaulted roof-frame of pointed section for the sake of lightness, are given rhythm, towards the outside, by a series of granite arcatures carried by columns which stand away from the wall, the capitals of which have a stereotyped vegetable decoration. Between the arches, medallions with hollow trefoiling, a typically Norman feature, decorate the corner-pieces.

On the garden side, however, there is a procession of most original small columns. The were turned, as is shown by their circular capitals with smooth bells, and strike the eye first of all because of their beautiful crimson colour. They were remade, at the time of the restorations, in Lucerne conglomerate. Ten or so of the original columns still exist, however. They have the same shape and look the same, but are made of a different material, a fossil-bearing limestone imported from England, from Purbeck or from Battle, north of Hastings in the county of Sussex. This luxurious stone, used on the other side of the Channel on prestigious sites (cathedrals of Canterbury, Durham, Salisbury...) is in its natural state of a discreet greyish ochre. it has the peculiarity of taking on, when polished, superb tones ranging from blood red to deep bronze green. One of the old columns actually shows a colour tending towards a greenish metallic finish. We can thus imagine that the cloister originally had more shimmering and subtle colours than the present slightly glaring monochrome effect.

But the main interest of this colonnade is above all in its arrangement in quincunx: the two rows of supports are here not twinned in pairs, but offset by a half-interval. It is sometimes said that the cloister of Mont-Saint-Michel is the only example of this system. That is true today, but old engravings show that other Norman cloisters were built on the same principle in the middle ages: Saint-Vigor de Bayeux and Saint-Pierre-sur-Dive in the Calvados, Saint-Evroult in the Orne... It appears that these cloisters, which have since disappeared, were more recent than

The cloisters: overall view and crossed arches.

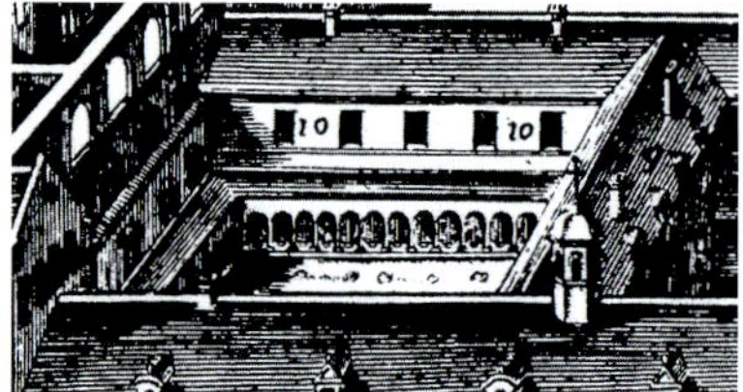
Cloister of Saint-Vigor at Bayeux.

Cloister of Saint-Pierre-sur-Dive.

Cloister of Saint-Evroult.
Engravings from "Monasticum Gallicanum".

that of Mont-Saint-Michel, which may have served as model for them.

This device with no known precedent nevertheless fits in well with the architectural traditions of the duchy. It represents the interpretation in three dimensions of superimposed series of arcatures, often used in surface decoration in Norman Romanesque art: we can see examples of it at Evreux, Saint-Etienne de Caen, Graville-Sainte-Honorine, Vatierville, Courcie, Broglie, Routot...The same theme is also to be seen in the interior of the refectory of Saint-Wandrille. The Normans exported it to England after the 1066 conquest (Winchester, Canterbury, Rochester, Worcester, Malmesbury, etc.), and even to their Sicilian domains.

The usefulness of this arrangement has been interpreted in various ways. Viollet-le-Duc, thinking as a reasoning technician, wrote: "It is obvious that this system of small columns laid out in a diamond pattern is better capable of resisting the thrust or the movement of a roof-frame than the method using twin columns, for the diagonal arches present a double resistance to these thrusts, brace the structure and make the two rows of columns interdependent. Besides, there is no need to repeat that a weight resting on three feet is more stable than if it is resting on two or on four. Now, the gallery the Mont-Saint-Michel cloister is nothing but a series of tripods..."

To that we may add that the arrangement in quincunx makes possible a degree of lightness considerably superior to that which would be offered by the traditional system. The latter creates an alternation, in the wall carried by the columns, hollow masses (the arches) and solid masses (the cornerstones). The arrangement adopted by the architect of La Merveille, on the other hand, produces far more hollow than solid, each cornerstone of one side of the gallery being cut away behind because it corresponds to an arch on the other side. In total, over the whole of the cloister, the saving in materials is considerable.

Stability and lightness: this double requirement can here be regarded as a necessity, since the cloister is built on the extrados of the vaults of the floor below. However, one should not overestimate these technical considerations. The galleries support neither a stone vault nor an upper storey, and the span of their roof-frameis very modest. The cloister is thus light enough not to cause any problems of seating.

In fact the real interest of this arrangement lies elsewhere. The offsetting of the two rows of columns made it possible to avoid the corner blocks which are customary in traditional cloisters, which make such a strong statement of the quadrangular structure and create in the four corners a strong caesura in the apprehension of the space as a totality. Additionally, the eye can find no rhythmically recurring element on the garden side, the wall has neither buttress not carving. One's gaze is therefore attracted solely by the uninterrupted sequence of the two rows of columns, off-

Canterbury cathedral. Crossed arches ("Dictionnaire..." by Viollet-le-Duc).

The offsetting of the two rows of columns avoids an interruption of the rhythm in the corners.

set by a half interval, accentuated still further by the impression of acceleration produced by the view of the galleries in perspective. Through this dynamic effect, the cloister is perceived as a symbolically circular space.

It thus evokes, in conformity with medieval traditions, the earthly garden of Paradise of the book of Genesis, also pointed up by the idealized vegetation of the carving. But the cloister also represents, because of its square plan, the celestial Jerusalem of the end of time, which the book of Revelation describes as a city of precious stones. The choice of a high-priced material for the columns expressed this identification with the celestial city, as did the glittering of the polychrome decoration of the carvings, and of the brilliant glazed tiles which were the original roofing (the present roof of rustic schist is a misinterpretation from this point of view).

In this enclosed garden, hanging in the sky, the beginning and end of the Creation are thus symbolically telescoped, abolishing duration and summing up in its completeness the perfection of the divine work, from Alpha to Omega.

The carved decoration plays its part in the completeness of the place. Carried out in fine Caen limestone, a noble material exported as far as England for the construction of the Tower of London, we must imagine it painted in bright colours, of which a few traces still exist, especially in the south gallery.

The carving which covers the corner pieces and runs as a frieze the whole length of the galleries stands out in strongly detached relief from depressions carved into the stone. This virtuoso work makes the stalks and leaves vibrate on a background of shadow: it would be possible to string a thread behind the interlaced plants of the northern frieze along the whole length of the gallery.

We shall not here undertake the decoding of the complex meaning of these carvings, which through the use of storiated figures and learned symbols sums up, clockwise, the history of the Creation, the Fall, and the Redemption. This reading will be presented in detail in a future work. One thing, however, should be noted here. The themes of vegetation

Vegetable whirlwind.

which make up the essential content of the decoration of the cloister have often been looked at through the beautiful pages which Emile Mâle dedicated to the sculptors of the XIIth century: "In the first days of spring, they go into the forests of the Ile-de-France, where humble plants are beginning to pierce the earth. The bracken, rolled up on itself like a powerful spring, and still covered with a downy fuzz, but, along the banks of the streams, the arum lily is already on the point of unfolding. They cull the buds, the leaves which are going to open, and regard them with this tender and impassioned curiosity..." This naturalist attitude, which impregnates the art of the Sainte Chapelle, of the cathedrals of Paris and even more so of Reims, was completely unknown to the artists who made the cloister of Mont-Saint-Michel. Despite what has sometimes been written, the vegetation represented in the galleries does not show the flora of the region: it is completely imaginary and constitutes free variations on the theme of the vine of Christ. Perhaps we should seek the origins of this art, which is still Romanesque in spirit, in the traditions of the other side of the English Channel.

Norman Gothic architecture, from the beginning of the XIIth century, used carved vegetation to decorate wall surfaces. It is usually a matter of large rosaces, such as can be seen in the cathedrals of Dol, of Sées, of Bayeux, or of Coutances, and at the entrance of the chapter hall of Hambye. But, with the possible exception of the little church of Norrey-en-Bessin, slightly more recent, this carving nowhere attains the richness of invention and the mastery of execution to be found in the cloister of Mont-Saint-Michel.

This admirable work is signed. Three names are engraved on a corner piece of the south gallery: Das (Dom) Garin, a monk who probably conceived the symbolic programme, and Mag (Magister) Roger and Jehan, laymen and presumably sculptors. They finished their work in 1228: that date marks the end of the great worksite of La Merveille.

East gallery. The graceful vintner, hammered at the time of the Revolution, was almost completely remade around 1880.

Abandoned foundation structures of the third building of La Merveille around 1690.

THE CONSTRUCTIONS OF ABBOT RICHARD

In fact, as we have seen, it was intended to build a third building on the west side. The gigantic foundations, which still exist, were put into effect in the second quarter of the XIIth century by abbot Richard Trustin (1237-1264). But very soon the work was abandoned, because of a total reorganization of the access to the monastery.

The entrance to the abbey used to be at the foot of the western walls, that is on the opposite side from the village, which stretched on the south-east slopes of the rock. At the time only the abbey was fortified: the village, which was not surrounded by ramparts, was without defence in case of attack and would have offered to enemy troops a base and quarters at the very foot of the walls of the monastery.

Now, these early years of the XIIIth century were a time when, stimulated by the royal engineers, the art of fortification was the subject of extensive theoretical consideration, which later took the form of considerable progress in defensive construction. It is possible without being too imprudent to put forward the idea that the conquest of Normandy by Philippe Auguste in 1204 was the event which set in motion very important military developments at Mont-Saint-Michel, which brought together in a rational relationship the defences of the village and those of the abbey.

The decision was thus taken, in the years 1240-1250, to surround the little community with an enclosing wall and to transfer the entrance to the monastery to the east so that its defences should constitute the command post, as it were the keep, of the external fortifications. In 1256, a royal subsidy contributed to the carrying-out of these major works.

All that, of course, made necessary a total reorganization of the monastic buildings and of traffic within the abbey. The project for the western building of La Merveille called for a court-room on the ground floor, communicating as custom demanded with the Romanesque entrance. The transfer of the entrance gates to the other end of the monastery meant that this idea had to be abandoned; the point is that the hall of justice must be open to the public; it must therefore be built where the new entrance is, on the eastern side.

Abbot Richard Turstin therefore had a two-storey building erected to the south-east of the chancel of the cathedral. It was finished in 1257, and contained a porters' lodge and above that the court-room (hall of "la Belle Chaise"). The new entrance gate, built in the east wall, is a broad opening with a crown, with rich mouldings, the tympanum of which is decorated with niches and with hollowed trefoiled medallions. It gives access to the ground floor, a broad hall traditionally known as the "Hall of Guard". Its floor rises in successive levels following the escarpment of the rock; the three bays of groined vaulting, which constitute its roof, follow these changes of level: the difference in height between the lowest, on the south, and the floor of the upper storey made it possible to build in a mezzanine space, serving both as a watch post for the porters' lodge and an antechamber for the court-room.

The Hall of Guard was the reception point for pilgrims and visitors, who were then directed to the various buildings which, outside the enclosure, were accessible to them. A broad door in the east wall led to the Almonry, on the ground floor of La Merveille. Another, on the west side, opened on to a monumental open staircase, the "Grand Degré", which, following along the foundation buildings of the chancel and the south arm of the transept, then passes above the ossuary and ends at a platform at the level of the church, on the southern side of the nave. There is to be found the new main entrance of the abbey church: these transformations have turned the old western square into a simple service courtyard.

The unfinished project for La Merveille comprised, apart from the court-room, a large infirmary on the first floor. Richard Turstin decided to build it on the south-west corner of the monastery, above the building put up a century earlier by abbot Robert de Thorigny. What had origi-

State of the south-west building around 1390. Note the defensive arrangement of the superstructures and the size of the openings.

Above the Hall of Guard, the superb hall of Belle Chaise, the abbey court, was restored in 1994. The panelling has been ornamented with a decor inspired by the hall of the Fleurs-de-Lys(see photos pages 24 and 42).

nally been the roof space was replaced by a storey with groined vaulting, supporting a crenellated terrace on the same level as the western square of the abbey church.. The ancient illustrated documents show that this whole building at the time was pierced by high mullioned windows, not unlike those of La Merveille. These openings, too big for walls which received the enormous thrust of a Romanesque barrel vault, contributed to the weakening of masonry which was already sorely tried by the excess weight of an additional storey: the building finally collapsed in 1818.

The third hall planned in the never-realized building of La Merveille should have been a chapter hall. Richard Turstin gave up the idea of building it, and the hall of the Promenoir which was used for this purpose in Romanesque times was to keep its old function until the XVIIth century. This abandonment is evidence of the decline of Benedictine spirituality, at a time when a renewed religious feeling was spreading, freed from the feudal spirit and incarnated in the mendicant orders, the Franciscans and Dominicans. The constructions which were undertaken in the abbey during the following century were essentially civil buildings - abbot's lodgings and fortifications - which we have already presented in the first chapters of this book (see pages 12, 13, 14).

THE FLAMBOYANT GOTHIC CHANCEL

On September 20th 1421, when the Hundred Years' War was raging, the Romanesque chancel of the church, built four centuries earlier, collapsed. The uncertainties of war meant that it took twenty-five years to organize and finance the reconstruction, which started only in 1446.

The initiative for this reconstruction is due to abbot Guillaume d'Estouteville (1444-1482), an outstanding personage and holder of very important offices, espe-

The chancel. Exterior view from the south-west.

cially that of archbishop of Rouen. With his impetus behind it, the work at first proceeded at a smart pace, since in 1452 the pillars of the great arcades and the radiating chapels were built. But the work was then interrupted and was not to be re-started until 1500 by abbot Guillaume de Lamps (1500-1511)who built the chancel up to the level of the sills of the high windows. His brother, Jean de Lamps, finished the construction in 1521, exactly a century after the collapse of the original chancel. However, the original plan was faithfully respected right until the laying of the last stone, which means that today we can admire a perfectly homogeneous result.

Crypt of the Big Pillars. Note the extreme virtuosity with which the ribs fall in tangential penetration, characteristic of the flamboyant style.

The overall structure was determined by the conservation of the Romanesque foundation building: in fact, the XIth-century chancel collapsed down to the level of the transept pillars; the Romanesque crypt is thus largely re-usable and will form the kernel of the Gothic crypt (the Romanesque elements preserved inside the XVth-century masonry were discovered in 1964). On the basis of these remains, the architect's project included the addition of circumferential compartments to support the radial chapels of the chancel, which was built at the same level as the transept.

The low level is known by the very explicit name of the crypt "des Gros Piliers" (crypt of the Big Pillars). It is a dark, austere hall, encumbered by enormous cylindrical piers (6 metres [20 feet] in circumference!), and is lent animation only by the prismatic profile of the ribs of the vaulting, which create a harsh interplay of light and shade. This carefully finished, energetic and powerful architecture arouses no religious feelings, and indeed the crypt is not a place where the cult is practised. The peripheral compartments have no liturgical appointments (credenzas, piscinas or chests), and the windows are fitted with window-seats (stone benches in the embrasure, a device used only in civil architecture).

In reality, this crypt had a triple function. It was first and foremost a supporting structure: each of the piers supports one of the pillars of the chancel, and the twin shafts in the centre bear the weight of the high altar. It was also a point of passage between the various departments of the monastery. There are doors opening on all sides: on the west, a passage leads to the Saint-Martin crypt; on the south-west, a spiral staircase gives direct access to the high church; a neighbouring door allows one to reach the abbot's lodging via a bridge passing above the Grand-Degré; on the east there is communication with the entrance building, and on the north with the porch of La Merveille, which serves the Guest Hall and the enclosure.

But more than anything else, the crypt of the Big Pillars is the antechamber to the court-room, Belle-Chaise, which occupies the first floor of the entrance building. One can imagine the state of mind of the accused, waiting to appear before the high justice of the abbot, in this labyrinthine and oppressive "waiting room"!...

Keystones of the vaults of the chancel: arms of France, Saint Michael conquering the dragon, arms of the abbey and of the abbot Jean le Veneur (1524-1543).

Above, the chancel rises as a superb volume, all verticality and light. The plan makes an apse of nine bays - two in the straight portion on each side, and five in the rounded part - surrounded by an ambulatory on to which open five radiating chapels around the semi-circle and two rectangular chapels of two bays' length, one on the south and the other on the north.

The elevation comprises three levels. Diamond-shaped piers support very high arcading opening on to the ambulatory. Above, the gallery of the triforium admits exterior light through a wealth of glazed openings. Finally, the very high windows occupy the whole surface of the wall below the compartments of the groined vaulting.

The ensemble is very unadorned and has no carvings. Animation is given only by the flamboyant cut of the windows and the parapet of the triforium, and above all by the strongly emphasized part played by the mouldings, which are not interrupted either by rings or by capitals. The long mouldings which cover the pillars confer the greatest possible slimness on them, and fine columns spring from the floor in one bound to the keystones 25 metres [80 feet] higher. The mullions of the windows are in line with those of the triforium, and the continuity suggested by this between the two levels of piercing gives the impression that the whole structure, above the arcades, is an immense cage of light. All this graphic backdrop draws the eye towards the great upper windows, towards the light, towards the sky.

This masterpiece of airy delicacy is solidly help in place on the outside by a battery of elegant flying buttresses whose function is to receive and absorb the thrust of the vaults. Those of the straight parts send up two arches, one above the other, while those of the rounded part have only one. The abutments, high walls raised on the masonry separating the radial chapels, hide their strength beneath an appearance of lightness, produced by the transparency of a network of delicate piercing. The pinnacles, which were all remade during the restorations, replaced the original crowns, which represented angels playing musical instruments.

It is worth noting that the westernmost flying buttresses are crossed by arches at right angles to their own, abruptly ending in stones left in abeyance. This detail reveals the original project's ambition to rebuild the entire church in the flamboyant style; these same flying buttresses were also to buttress the vaulting that it was intended to build on the arms of the new transept. The fact that the project ran out of steam has fortunately allowed us to preserve the superb Romanesque parts of the church!

A close examination of the construction of this flamboyant chancel leaves us full of admiration in the face of the perfection of its execution. The quality of the solid geometry shows up in the spring of the vaulting of the crypt: the lines of the ribs which come to rest gently on the pillars in tangential penetration cross and intermingle with an astonishing virtuosity. In the chancel, the refinement of the gradation of the mouldings and bases reveals consummate artistry. We must also admire, on the exterior, the unusual mastery with which the arches of the flying buttresses are

Interior of the chancel: soaring verticality.

set up: the arches, which leave the abutments in *tas de charge* from the lines of the courses, pass gradually to an oblique bonding so that when they arrive at the thrust-point of the vaulting they present joints which are perpendicular to it.

This work of architecture of the highest order is markedly different from the great achievements of the Norman flamboyant style: the cathedral of Evreux, the church of Saint-Ouen of Pont-Audemer, or the parts of Rouen cathedral executed by the architect Guillaume Pontis, show an exuberant and tormented spirit which, in Germain Bazin's poetic words,"transforms a monument into a sort of cave with thousands of sculptured convolutions in which all architectonic form is submerged..."

By contrast, the Gothic chancel of Mont-Saint-Michel forms part of the classic tradition of the great age of the cathedrals of the XIIIth century. Its plan is that of the chancel of Reims, and its interior elevation, inspired by that of Saint-Ouen of Rouen (XIVth-century) carries on the essential accents already present in the chancel of the cathedral of Amiens. This does not mean, however, that it does not possess a number of original aspects. The extreme upward extension and the narrowness of the bays, for one thing, is certainly as much the result of deliberate choice as of the need to re-use the Romanesque foundation levels. Again, the triforium offers an extremely rare particularity: it does not pass through the pillars but goes round behind them. The system gives the outer wall a broken line, following the line of the mural gallery, the openings of which can be glazed. This device exists in only three other monuments, of the south of France, dating from the XIIIth and XIVth centuries: the cathedrals of Limoges, Clermont and Narbonne. One sees that the architect of the Mount, to avoid weakening the pillars while at the same time admitting yet more light, was able to find references which were distant both in time and space.

All in all, what are we to make of the thinking which inspired this highly-skilled master? The ultimate aim of his work is clear. By the closely controlled use of an architectural vocabulary which was as classical as it was eclectic, he has turned the chancel into a treatise in stone reduced to the essential: the vertical ascent of the gaze, drawn by the light. This is a graphical treatment of the same symbolic planning of space which had been thought up by the XIth-century architect when he designed a church built as a staircase.

On the upper arch of a flying buttress, the famous "lace staircase" leads to the gutter which crowns the wall of the chancel.

1023-1521: from the start of work on the construction of the church to the finishing of the chancel, the abbey church of Mont-Saint-Michel communicates the same message to us!

THE MODERN ERA

There is not much to say about the work carried out on the monument since the XVIth century. After a period of decadence, the abbey was united in 1622 to the congregation of Saint-Maur, a reformed Benedictine movement which grouped together a large number of French monasteries.

The new monks made curious use of the medieval buildings. In 1629, they moved into La Merveille, abandoning the other buildings to the prisoners (since Louis XI the Mont-Saint-Michel had been a royal prison) and to the personnel of the military government. They regrouped the various monastic services around the cloister, partitioned the great refectory and divided it into three floors to turn it into their dormitory (the restorations of the end of the XIXth century have happily effaced the traces of this ludicrous arrangement). Their refectory and the kitchen were transferred into the Guest Hall: the XIIIth-century kitchen was transformed into a warming-room and a new floor was built on top of it to be used as a library; the old Romanesque dormitory was converted into a map library and recreation room, and the little building up against it on the north into latrines. To simplify traffic between the enclosure and the church, and to make supply of provisions easier, the two superposed apsidioles of the north transept were dismantled, and a large straight stone staircase was built in the porch of the Guest Hall.

A plan of the following century (1776) shows us the sad usage that was made of the venerable sanctuaries of the foundation levels: Notre-Dame-des-Trente-Cierges is shown as a wine-cellar, the little room which precedes it as a beer-cellar, the Aquilon as a cider cellar. The Saint-Etienne chapel became a storage-place for firewood, Saint-Martin a horse-driven mill!...

But the most interesting work of the Benedictines of Saint-Maur is without doubt the present façade of the abbey church. In 1776, a fire ravaged the church, which suffered considerable damage. The lower part of the nave, in particular, threatened to fall in ruins, and the decision had to be taken to demolish the three western bays to avoid their collapse. A new façade was then built to close off the shortened

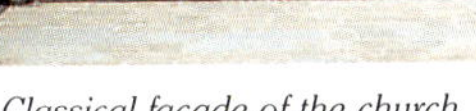

Classical façade of the church.

Neo-medieval capitals of the façade.

nave. It is classical in shape and structure, and in perfect proportion. Its slightly cold, dry look is luckily softened by a fine patina and golden lichens whose warm colours shine in the afternoon sun.

This façade is remarkable above all for the series of six capitals which crown the embedded half-columns of the first level. Where one would expect to find the soberness of the classical orders, one discovers corbeils with a complex decor, inspired by the Romanesque capitals of the church, with corner-scrolls, palm-leaves, masks and interlacing. The one on the right shows a curious figure of a pilgrim with a cornet on his shoulder directly copied from the exterior carvings of the Gothic chancel.. Now, we are in 1780: Chateaubriand is twelve years old and the Romantic movement which will bring about the re-discovery of the middle ages will not become important until half a century later ("The Battle of Hernani", 1830). Thus we have here evidence of an extremely early intrusion into French architecture of medieval historiography.

From 1792 to 1863 the deserted abbey was converted into a prison. The sordid conversions which were made at that time were happily done away with at the time of the restorations: a wooden floor halfway up the height of the nave for storage of stocks of straw (the prisoners made hats), a floor of cells (the huts) built above the galleries of the cloister, evisceration of the walls of Notre-Dame-sous-Terre to establish communication between the north and south buildings... The only remaining evidence of this sinister epoch is the capstan-crane installed below the Grand Degré staircase for hoisting up provisions.

In 1834, a gigantic fire broke out in the church, causing considerable damage to the masonry. Mérimée, who came to the Mount on a tour of inspection in 1841, found the sanctuary in such a state of dilapidation that he compared the stones to "sugar-lumps soaked in water". To hide these ravages, the walls were masked by a granitelike rendering and the nave covered by a sham Gothic vault of plaster around 1860 (traces of this dummy vaulting can still be seen on the inner side of the façade).

Such is the sad reality that the architect Edouard Corroyer found in 1872, when he was sent to Mont-Saint-Michel to prepare the restorations.

THE RESTORATIONS

By a decree of April 20th 1874, the abbey of Mont-Saint-Michel was put under the control of the Historic Monuments service. Considerable funds were made available at the time to make the restorations possible. The history of these restorations reflects he evolution of the theoretical thinking of the service about the work carried out by the successive architects-in-chief.

The first three, Edouard Corroyer (1872-1889), Victor Petitgrand (1889-1898) and Paul Gout (1898-1923) were pupils of Viollet-le-Duc (Petitgrand via the intermediary of his teacher Anatole de Baudot, himself a disciple of the famous master). Their activities, especially where Corroyer and Petitgrand are concerned, show evidence of the "Viollet-le-Ducian" doctrine expounded in the celebrated "Reasoned dictionary of French architecture from the XIth to the XVIth century". "Restoring an edifice is not maintaining it, repairing it or re-making it, it is re-establishing it in a state of completeness which may never have existed at any given moment..." The esthetic basis of this theory is the concept of "unity of style". Obviously, , all that gives great freedom of manoeuvre to the architects in charge of restorations, in order that their projects should form part of a coherent historiographic reading of the monument.

The finest example is the spire executed by Petitgrand from 1890 to 1897. The main structure of the Romanesque tower, built by abbot Bernard de Bec in 1136, had been preserved, despite numerous fires and additions which had made the masonry fragile: the construction in 1609 of an additional storey, overhanging the vaulting of the original stack, then of a heavy roof supporting an open campanile (replaced in 1776 by an enormous four-faced roof). Petitgrand, working from the rock upwards, rebuilt as new the great pillars of the transept crossing, then the Romanesque storey above, of which not one old stone was preserved and of which he slightly changed the look; he rebuilt the XVIIth-century level but gave it a medieval look, inspired by the XIIth-century bell-towers of his native Cal-

Victor Petitgrand's spire makes the silhouette of the Mount splendidly complete.
Left: view from the east, right: view from the west

vados, and topped it with a high, four-faced roof-frame; finally, on top of all that, he placed a neo-Gothic spire in embossed copper, thus reproducing, with one storey fewer, the one which Viollet-le-Duc had executed at Notre-Dame de Paris in 1857. Last of all, the "Archangel", by Frémiet, was fixed to the summit on August 6th 1897.

This superposition of elements from diversified periods and places of reference is an expression of the ideal Mont-Saint-Michel, synthesizing the art of the middle ages in a daring abridgment. It is indeed true that the miniature from the "Très Riches Heures du duc de Berry" attests the existence at the end of the XIVth century of a Gothic spire on the monument; a second one, also very tall and thin, had been put up in 1509 and, according to an eye-witness (Auguste de Thou, who came on pilgrimage in 1581) it was crowned by a gilded statue of the archangel Saint Michael.

The overall silhouette of the Mount defined by Petitgrand resuscitates its old arrangement in an extremely monumental interpretation. The architect designed it with particular care for its proportionality. The point of the spire exactly doubles the original height of the rock (i.e. the floor level of the church), and the ratio between the latter and the height of the openwork belvedere of the spire corresponds precisely to the Golden Number (see the cover of this book). The ensemble is not far removed from the shape of the Mount as Viollet-le-Duc had reconstructed it, in a beautiful engraving in his "Dictionary..."

Petitgrand's successor, Paul Gout, was appointed in 1898. He is indisputably the greatest architect-in-chief of Mont-Saint-Michel, and also its principal historian: the big reference-book which he left us remains irreplaceable to this day. Although he too was a pupil of Viollet-le-Duc, he presents in his works a body of doctrine which is a radical break with the conceptions of his predecessors. He is a violent critic of the principale of unity of style, and treats the work of reconstitution of the parts which have disappeared very severely; for him they are "" developments - sometimes imaginary - given to a theme provided by a few fragments of architecture or a few formless ruins...". His conception of his mission is summed up thus: "Restoration must never, as a principle, depart from the task of preserving a state of the edifice prior to mutilations or transformations which have no definite link with its history or its artistic character." The desire for prudent authenticity expressed by Paul Gout is accompanied by his taking into account the very appearance of the materials. He recommends, when old masonry is being restored, that as many original pieces as possible should be preserved, even if they are "chipped, worn or layered", as long as they can still fulfil their constructional rôle. However, Paul Gout does not make any objection to the discreet use of contemporary techniques, if they are able to contribute to effective preservation: reinforced concrete, for instance, which is frequently found in his work. These are on the whole pretty modern ideas, and Paul Gout's successors, Pierre Paquet (1923-1929), Bernard Haubold (1929-1933) and Ernest Herpe, the restorer of the monastery living quarters (1933-1957) will not depart from them. They contain in embryonic form, the principles which will underlie the 1964 Venice Charter, a document which lays down a precisely defined international doctrine for the preservation of historic monuments.

The medieval Mont-Saint-Michel as Viollet-le-Duc imagines it.

An important era in the history of the restorations of the abbey is then marked by the long reign (1957-1983) of Yves-Marie Froidevaux. The brilliant architect worked on the crypts and the Romanesque buildings, but above all on two outstandingly important sites.

The first was the restoration of the chapel Notre-Dame-sous-Terre in 1960-61. We saw above that this venerable sanctuary had in the XIth century been cluttered with masonry whose aim was to support the western parts of the Romanesque nave; the two little chancels had also been hidden by the foundations of the classical façade of the church in 1780; the north and south walls had been eviscerated during the prison period. Froidevaux reconstituted the missing sections of wall with such skill in his treatment of the surfaces (the "epidermis" he called it) that we are today unable to distinguish the XXth-century masonry from that of the Xth; he took down the massive Romanesque supporting structures which had become pointless since the disappearance of the three western bays of the nave; finally, he did away with the big XVIIIth-century wall which obstructed the two eastern compartments. The problem which first had to be solved was to provide a reliable support for the façade of the high church: to achieve this, Froidevaux buried in the vaulting, beneath the weight which was to be supported, two parallel girders of pre-stressed concrete (i.e. concrete reinforced by steel cables under tension); the five hundred tonne burden of the wall above was thus assumed by this invisible ladder, stretched like a gigantic spring, and the supporting wall could be removed without difficulty.

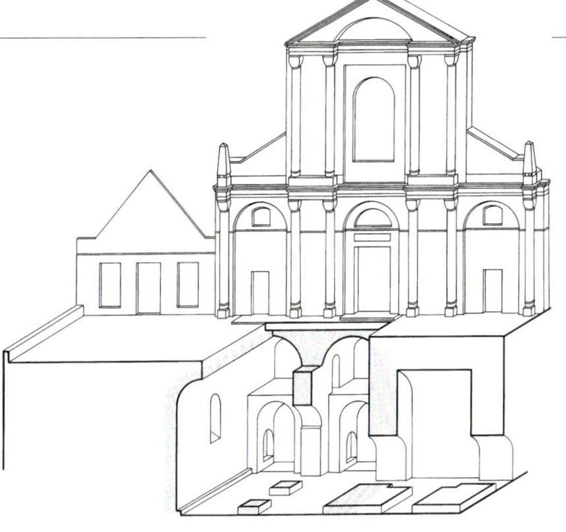

Position of the crypt of Notre-Dame-sous-Terre under the classical façade of the church.

This technologically advanced restoration, carried out with great skill and sensitivity, restored the crypt to its original volume. It remains a model of its type.

The other important work carried out by Froidevaux was the re-establishment of a garden in the cloister, on a sober and refined plan conceived by father Bruno de Senneville. To the same period belongs the replacement of the gallery roofs. After two successive roofs in glazed tiles, executed by Corroyer and Paul Gout,, Froidevaux chose a different material, a rustic-looking grey-green schist such as one sees on the traditional barns of the Cotentin. This affected humility is regrettable, in the context of this cloister which was conceived to represent the celestial Jerusalem of the Apocalypse, a city made of precious stones.

In fact, at this point we stumble over the weakness of the admirable and attractive work carried out by Yves-Marie Froidevaux. It is far too marked by the religious sensitivity arising from the Vatican II council, with which he is deeply impregnated. It is legitimate to question the appropriateness of cultivating a systematic severity, almost Cistercian in its nature, in the restoration of a monastery which for eight centuries had perpetuated the Cluniac tradition of pomp and splendour; the altars erected in the various chapels are, in this respect, just so many misinterpretations. Worse, the dismally coloured flagged floor laid in the refectory creates, because of its brutal lines in the floor, strongly emphasized false bays, whereas the XIIIth-century architect had conceived a unified space in which no rhythm should appear. One must hope that this arrangement shall one day become the object of a "derestoration".

The current works, carried out since 1983 by Pierre-André Lablaude, are a continuation of what went just before as far as the care taken with the appearance of the surfaces is concerned, where the artificial patina ensures that the eye is not shocked by the new sections. However, the philosophy behind them is very different. Apart from some spectacularly technical operations, such as the restoration, much reported in the media, of the statue of the Archangel in 1987, the re-creation of a vegetable garden on the vaulting of a cistern to the northeast of the chancel, or the clearing as part of the foundations of a Romanesque hall forgotten for seven centuries under the west terrace, the operations directed by M. Lablaude continue the tradition of the preceding century. They are in fact aimed at giving visitors to Mont-Saint-Michel a colour and an atmosphere arising from a historiographic and pedagogical conception of the site, using a free interpretation of the ancient reference documents.

In the village, for instance, frame houses have been rebuilt from scratch, not with their original appearance - which is in any case unknown - but in accordance with a plan inspired by the miniature of

The restorations of 1980-1990 are aimed at an overall look rather than the former state: terrace of the châtelet, roof of Belle-Chaise and kitchen garden recreated to the north-east of the chancel (photo Luigi Levak).

the "Très Riches Heures du duc de Berry" and the relief-map of the Invalides. Rather than archaeological truth, what is aimed at here is the overall impression.

In the abbey itself. the Saut-Gautier building has been given a roof like an upturned ship's hull, mounted on a "small wood" roof frame in the manner of Philibert Delorme. This execution is entirely the child of the architect's imagination: its only "scientific" justification is a rounded gable no doubt built in the second half of the XIXth century! However, for an observer situated on the western terrace, it contributes to a harmonious appreciation of the classical façade, and is a discreet reminder that the abbey did not come to a halt at the end of the middle ages.

The same applies to the superb panelled roof-frame, decorated with a pattern of fleurs-de-lys, installed in the hall of Belle-Chaise. No ancient document shows such a device, but this creation restores to the hall its rôle as a ceremonial space, linked to the display of the feudal power of the monastery. The painted decor, inspired by a mural rendering of the XIIIth century, discovered in 1962 in one of the western halls, indicates that the Mount was for a long time a site emblematic of the sacred legitimacy of the royal power.

The yet more daring gilded finials, brilliant and luxurious, with which the roof-ridges were adorned a few years ago, are not attested to in any ancient representation of the abbey. They nonetheless correspond to the appearance, shown in Gothic miniatures, of the visual tokens of places of power, châteaux and cathedrals. They are no misinterpretation on a monument which for centuries, in the minds of those who conceived it, was intended to be a representation of the celestial Jerusalem.

All these steps have called forth a variety of reactions, and they have sometimes been violently attacked. It seems very probable, however, that the passage of time will bring about their acceptance, as with Petitgrand's spire, which is today an inseparable element of the Mount's silhouette, famous all over the world, and no-one would now dream of questioning its legitimacy.

The restorations of Mont-Saint-Michel are not finished. Over more than a century they have beautified the site and given it a diversity of meanings. What will they be in a few decades' time? How will the Mount be interpreted at the opening of the third millennium? The answer is simple: as an organism which is still living and still able to respond to men's questions.

 - Imprimé en France par Gibert Clarey Imprimeurs (37)
I.S.B.N. 978-2-7373-6671-0 - Dépôt légal : mars 2015 - N° d'éditeur : 7775.02.0,7.03.16
www.editionsouestfrance.fr